# TURNING
# POINTS

25 inspiring stories from women
entrepreneurs who have turned
their careers and their lives around

Edited by Kate Cobb
**Forewords by Kay White and Joyce O'Brien**
With contributions from Rachel Rofé and Frederique Murphy

# PRAISE FOR THIS BOOK

"*Turning Points* is a riveting read!

These stories read like best selling fiction, yet they are real people facing unbelievable circumstances. These entrepreneurs have not only survived, but each has risen above her challenges like a phoenix! I found myself incredulous, and inspired by the courage and inner strength these women displayed. The resilience of the entrepreneurs featured in this book is humbling, and what's interesting to me is they did not go it alone. They credit the support of loved ones, teachers, mentors and coaches with giving them the strength and guidance to overcome their circumstances. If you are an entrepreneur, or consider yourself a 'survivor' in any way, this book is for you. Prepare to be lifted up!"

**Holli Thompson, health and nutrition coach, author and**
**broadcaster**
**www.NutritionalStyle.com**


"If you're stuck in a rut in your life, *Turning Points* is the book to read. Women entrepreneurs talk honestly and courageously about their biggest challenges and how they overcame them and share their learning with us so we can benefit."

**Dr Scott & Shannon Peck, co-authors of bestseller,**
***The Love You Deserve: A Spiritual Guide to Genuine Love,***
**www.ScottandShannonPeck.com**


"An absolutely unique, inspirational book! Filled with personal accounts of huge challenges overcome. These women are amazing!"

**Kimberly Smith, President,**
**Powerful Parents, Powerful Lives,**
**www.acesforlife.com**

"Real challenges overcome, real emotions along with buckets of good advice from the inspiring *Turning Points* women. Informative, insightful, compelling – this is the stuff of motivational literature."

**Cindy Prosor, Your Happiness Mentor,**
**www.OpeningDoorsWithin.com**

"If you are looking for inspiration and affirmation, excitement and incitement you can find it all in this eclectic mix of amazing stories from all walks of life. These 25 short action packed stories hang together as an inspiring quilt of different textures and contrasting tones. The common threads running through all of the Turning Points include self awareness, self belief and individuals becoming themselves."

**Claire-Marie Boggiano, chartered engineer,**
**business change and people development professional.**

"I've just read your book!! I am so glad that I did. So totally inspirational and motivational and testament to the inherent strength of women."

**Liz Field,**
**CEO Financial Services Skills Council, London**

"Rarely does a book find a way not only to take you on a personal life-changing journey, but also is able to give you shining examples of those who have gone before, to serve as guideposts shining their wisdom for you to light the pathway 'Home'. This is such a book. As you read each woman's journey, you will see with greater depth and understanding, the sacred journey within."

**Rose Cole, CNC, CNHP Natural health**
**and nutrition consultant, mentor,**
**www.RoseCole.com**

"If you're scared of going for your dream, then read the stories of these inspirational women. They all have an amazing positive perspective to share about their challenging experiences and there is so much to learn from them. Highly recommended."

**Cyndi Fine, from Stuck to Unstoppable — Mind Body Expert,**
**www.cyndifine.com**

"If you are planning on starting a business this is a must read! Real entrepreneurs giving you realistic accounts of their journey, the hardships and the joys. Packed full of wisdom."

**Johanna McClain,**
**Certified Business Coach and Certified Brand Strategist,**
**www.JohannaMcClain.com**

"This book shows how ordinary people can overcome great odds, get inspired, turn things round and achieve their goals. Fantastic reading!"

**Melissa Evans, The Guru of Implementation,**
**www.BrosheGroup.com**

"Talk about TURNING Points!! Every single one of these stories is a profound gift! Not only to women, not only to entrepreneurs but to ANYONE who is up against a wall and yearning for the kind of inspiration and motivation that will provide the key to breaking through into the light! I especially recommend the story by my colleague and friend Karin Volo – if her journey isn't about turning lemons into lemonade I don't know what is! Angels are among us – they are RIGHT here in this very book!"

**Amethyst Wyldfyre,**
**Destiny Mentor for the Empowered Messenger,**
**www.theempoweredmessenger.com**


"An amazing book! You will be inspired and motivated as you read the personal accounts and share what these women authors have learned. Fantastic!"

**Rae Luskin, the Healed Heart Expert, artist, teacher, activist**
**and the author of *Art From My Heart,***
**www.raeluskin.net**


"Any entrepreneur knows that when you take that risk to do what you love, there are days when you want to give up. Inspiring stories, like the amazing ones in this book, are what keep you going when all logic tells you to stop. This collection of tales of obstacles and overcoming is these women's generous gift to you; read it often and you will be inspired to reach levels in your business you previous thought impossible."

**Kristi Shmyr, The Goal Getting Ninja,**
**www.GoalNinjas.com**

First Published Great Britain 2011
by Summertime Publishing

ISBN:  978-1-904881-37-7

Design by Creationbooth - www.creationbooth.com

# DEDICATION

For Edna who faced her own Turning Points
with courage and who has been the role
model and inspiration for all of my life.

# ACKNOWLEDGEMENTS

I would like to acknowledge all the women I spoke to in the course of this project; whether they eventually chose to appear in this book or not, they all had a story to tell. All these women are living examples of courage and determination. They are an inspiration to all and give the proof that there are individuals in the world truly making a difference to others. With their help the world is a better place.

I would also like to thank my publisher, Jo Parfitt at Summertime Publishing, without whose encouragement and support this book would not have been possible.

# FOREWORDS

# Kay White

This inspirational, motivational and truly thought-provoking book sets out to share with its readers how each of the 25 women contributors, from all around the world, handled the situation in which they found themselves and what they learned along the way. They want you to avoid, as far as possible, experiencing the same pain, doubt and often life or sanity-threatening experiences. In reading their stories you're invited to stand powerfully upon these inspirational women's shoulders so you can move forward when you come up against your *own* Turning Points, your own forks-in-the-road.

What becomes crystal clear as you read *Turning Points* is that there's no going back. Once you come up against a Turning Point, and you will, gather yourself and discover that 'core of strength within you that survives all hurt'[1]. Every one of these stories will make you stop and realise that 'there but for a heartbeat' go I. When I read Tracy Neely's story, I welled up with emotion. It brought back to me my biggest (so far) Turning Point which occurred when I was just 16 years old. I was told I had 24 hours to live having been diagnosed with ovarian cancer. I was lucky. It was operable and then treatable and those 24 hours have already been extended by more than 30 amazing years though I'm unable to have children as a result of the treatment. Despite that life-changing result, I still choose to believe I'm truly lucky to have had the warning backache and to be cured. I grab and love my life more than you can ever know as a result of it. Making my business and career as a savvy and influential communication expert, I show professionals how to get noticed, promoted and rewarded as they go about their business, and my own book, *The A to Z of* Being Understood, came from another Turning Point. Someone asking me "when are you going to write some of this stuff down, Kay?" So I have. So have these 25 amazing women

Kay White, Communication Expert, England
Author of the Number 1 Bestseller
*The A to Z of Being Understood*
www.wayforwardsolutions.com

---

[1] *"The turning point in the process of growing up is when you discover the core of strength within you that survives all hurt."*
*Max Lerner, US Politician and Columnist 1902-1992*

# Joyce O'Brien

*Turning Points* will change your life. The stories will shock you, bring you to tears and then leave you inspired to create something much bigger in your own life. As I read, my jaw dropped at what the courageous women in these stories had been through. *Turning Points* will leave you wondering how you can look at life and your choices differently to support you in your vision of what your life could be. Yet, if you pick just one story that resonates with you, it could change your life. The authors hold out hope and possibility to all of us.

My own Turning Point came ten years ago when my husband and I were both diagnosed with late stage cancers. I was told nothing could be done to save me and he was given a 20-30 per cent chance of survival. We were likely going to die and leave our three-year-old little girl an orphan. I had a choice to make, I could either accept the fate I was given or I could choose to live.

My decision was to choose to live and by making this choice I became empowered. The devastation of this Turning Point became the biggest gift that I ever could have imagined. I left a successful career on Wall Street to share a message of hope, inspiration and 'how to' so that others can know it's possible for them to heal cancer and other illnesses. We've both been cancer free for ten years.

We each have a story to share – a gift for others to support them on their journey. Do you have a turning point that is a gift to share with others?  If so, please don't hold on to it. Share it, as these women have done, with those who are waiting for you. If you have yet to experience a turning point, maybe this book will become a turning point for you. In any case, please read on to be inspired and empowered and to know that anything is possible.

Joyce O'Brien, Speaker, Vitality Coach,
United States
Author of *Choose to Live, Our Journey from Late Stage Cancers to Vibrant Health*
http://www.JoyceOBrien.com
http://www.BeingCancerFree.com

# TABLE OF CONTENTS

# INTRODUCTION

Do you ever feel like giving up? That it is all too difficult and you can't go on? That it would just be easier to sit back and do nothing?

We've all felt like that at one time or another and particularly the authors in this book!

The stories in this book from the 25 women entrepreneurs are all true and recount the most significant Turning Point of their lives so far. You will read about the fear, anxiety and depression most we of us felt at some point and the subsequent evolution and positive development we have experienced as a result. The book tells the tale of how we got from where we were *then* to where we are now. You will journey with us as we recount what's happened to us in the past and what practical steps we took to turn the Turning Points to our advantage. This is a book to inspire and motivate you, to pick you up when you fall down, to energise you when you are feeling low and give you ideas when you have none.

## What is a Turning Point?

The Turning Point is literally the moment you turn your life around; when you realise your circumstances can't get any worse and in that instant, you pivot your life about by making the decision that you *will* change things for the better, even though you may not know how. Or it can be a blinding flash of light when everything suddenly falls into place and you know exactly that you have to change your life.

All of us will probably have several major Turning Points in our lives. If you're nodding then you probably already appreciate how many you've had and how far *you've* come through your own Turning Points.

The transition can be a very uncomfortable ride for a while and the difficulties we experience as we try to shift from the 'old me' to a new improved version are like the growing pains of a child, getting taller, getting wiser. I remember when I was at my Turning Point, and discovered I may face a life in a wheelchair, how I felt devastated, empty, the world crashed down and I began to think 'what's the point?'. The run up to the Turning Point is tough but once we make the turn, we enter a major growth stage in our lives, whether we recognise this at the time or not. After all, if we had no challenges to overcome in life, how could we appreciate our achievements?

## Why do we have Turning Points?

We need them to propel us forwards, to change the course of our lives and our careers so we can do bigger and better things. Sometimes we make these changes consciously and with a lot of forethought but more often than not we need that tap on the shoulder by the Universe to get us going. How many times have you looked back on an event which was painful, unbearable, or simply totally unexpected at the time, to realise that it was that very event that pushed you on to achieve the success you have had? If that hasn't happened to you yet, then it certainly will. As you will see in Beth's story, this is exactly what occurred as, out of the blue, she discovered she had 48 hours to give up her home, family, friends, career and prepare to move from the US to Korea.

*Turning Points are essential.*

## Why don't we see Turning Points as positive?

Turning Points are major positive transformational moments in our lives but we often don't see this at the time. It's a shame we can't recognise and embrace this as they come along. It would save us a lot of pain and heartache, wouldn't it? One of the common themes in this book is the authors' belief that everything happens for a reason, so we think that the heartaches are there to help us grow, to be more discerning in our future choices and to propel us towards the life we are meant to be leading on this planet. We believe that everyone has a unique role to play and that many people are now searching to discover their path. Our Turning Points actually point the way to the next step but we are often blinded by fear, or lack of confidence, or lack information about what to do next; and that applies to all of us, even those of us who *know* that Turning Points are fantastic learning opportunities!

# Fear

We may dress it up in all sorts of other words like 'uncertainty', 'nervousness', 'reluctance' and so on, but basically we are scared of change and the unknown. As a general rule, human beings don't like change and find it stressful because it threatens their comfort and security and, however bad a current situation is, many choose to put up with it rather than go through the upheaval of moving on. As Julia says in her story, even though she knew all about the theory of change management she wasn't able to apply that clinically to her own situation and bypass her emotions.

When our basic survival is threatened, as in Karin's and Linda's stories, it is perfectly normal to feel fear, both for ourselves and for those closes to us. When Aleksandra stood on the doorstep that day with her two-year old son facing homelessness, she was literally unable to move because of the fear. If your health is threatened like Tracy's and my story, then the fear paralyses you for a time. When the fabric of your family life, what you have been brought up with, is shaken or removed from you as in Frederique's and Janet's stories, it is pretty tough to face up to the unknown and carry on.

But carry on we must and we have to find a way through our fears and our anxieties and use them as a trampoline to the next step.

# Lack of confidence

We all experience confidence issues every now and again, moments when we doubt a new project or take a deep breath before plunging into a risk. But as all the authors in this book are women, we share a tendency to be extremely good at being hard on ourselves and very good at knocking our *own* confidence from the inside as we criticise and put ourselves down! Ann's story is a typical example of a highly experienced and skilled woman faced with ruin who couldn't see her own potential – it took someone else to point it out to her.

We are always subjected to outside voices who question our judgement or our ability to embark on a new venture or who want us to stay in our old self. Couple this with our *own* inner voice and you have a powerful mix, as Nicole recounts in her story.

We may allow ourselves to be governed by the past for a time because our experience has knocked our self confidence and our basic belief in ourselves. When you read Kelly's story and see her exhausted and helpless at the effect on her family of her then-husband's drug addiction, you will understand why we become wary of others and our own ability to choose wisely. Ana's story of financial ruin echoes this.

Perhaps we have been so 'protected' from knowing what we want that we don't know who we are. We feel trapped in our role, a role we have either chosen for ourselves or that society has chosen for us. Look at Natalie's and Sarah's stories, where they both talk about having to find themselves as individual human beings.

Our lack of confidence and lack of self belief means we prevent ourselves achieving all we are capable of. We miss out on so much because we don't feel confident enough to put ourselves forward for promotion or apply for a better job, or we don't believe that we could make a success of our own business, so we don't even try. If you allow the negative gremlins in your head to dominate your thinking, you are not on the way to having the life you want (and deserve) but it is often lack of confidence which stops us seizing the moment and seeing the challenge in it.

## Lack of knowledge

We put emotional blocks in our way and allow them to stop us moving forward. But sometimes the practical tools we need may also be missing. We don't know any other way and lack information about possible alternative routes. In that moment we may not be able to see we have any options. We may have ideas of what we could do, but don't know how to start. Louise wanted to make a change but she was in a new country with small children and Anna found a whole new business opportunity that enabled her to help others. Both lacked knowledge when they set out.

# HOW CAN WE MAKE THE MOST OF OUR TURNING POINTS?

Given that these Turning Points are so influential in the total story of our lives, we need the keys to make the most of the experiences, preferably as they are happening, rather than after the event as we all write about in this book.

**Three keys to making the most of your Turning Point**

### 1) Know yourself

The more you know and understand yourself and what 'makes you tick', the better able you are to ride the difficult and challenging times and see them as learning experiences rather than blocks.

As Anne writes in her story, she realised that it was essential to be honest with herself before she could move on even though that meant owning up to the shame, disgust and self-pity she felt. Christina writes of how she was driven by a search for self respect and respect from others and that this gave her her way forward.

Once you know yourself you are in a better place to take responsibility for your choices and your actions. You know that YOU are the writer-director of your own play, that the situations you encounter are the script you have written and that the other people in your life are simply actors you have invited to join in the action. Taking responsibility means not blaming others and releases incredible creative energy. This is the pivotal point in Tara's story.

## 2) Get support

It's tough to go through this on your own. Even if you have close family and friends around you, it isn't always possible or appropriate to discuss your own 'dark night of the soul' with them or just to chew over your ideas. And, at that bleakest of moments, our own vision is clouded and blurred and it's hard to see our *own* way through.

As we share our learning points with you, you will read what steps we have taken to make the future happen. For example, Susan had a coach who prompted her 'aha' moment, though maybe not in the way the coach intended. Jo was given some concrete advice by her mentor and this helped her transform the way she was doing business.

Coaches and mentors are, of course, both totally impartial and also 100 per cent biased – as outsiders to us, they have no agenda of their own yet they are completely 'there' for us and encourage us 100 per cent – so they are vital allies in our change process. They will also hold us accountable and this is very motivating.

## 3) Amass knowledge

To make that next step forwards, you may need to do research, learn new skills, teach yourself something, ask questions of others. If you are prepared to invest in yourself and your learning, then amazing vistas open up. Lori found this at a training event when just hearing a quotation pierced her darkness and Rachel discovered it when attending an empowering workshop.

These keys can open the door for us to go through and into another world. We share our 'wisdom along the way' in each of our stories in the hope that this wisdom will assist you in your own quest and that the 'resources to rave about' will provide you with sources of information, inspiration and support which may be new to you and may help you find a new key for your own door.

Good luck

I wish you the very best of Turning Points as you move forward, your way.

Kate Cobb
Director
Moving Forward YOUR Way
France
8 July 2011
www.movingforwardyourway.com
kate@movingforwardyourway.com

# WHO SHOULD READ THIS BOOK?

Anyone who is facing a challenge, feels stuck, wants to make changes, is lacking in 'get up and go', who is at a transition point in their lives. Anyone who needs to be reminded of the resilience of the human spirit and be uplifted by it. In fact, anyone!

If you ever feel that you can't do something you want or feel you *need* to do, then read the stories of the women here who overcame great odds to get where they are today. They too often thought of giving up, but they didn't; they are role models of persistence, determination and sheer guts. What they have done, they have done for themselves, for their families and for their communities, and their achievements are colossal. We all have the potential for acts of great courage.

# FROM INCARCERATION TO INSPIRING OTHERS

## *KARIN'S STORY*
## *INSPIRING YOUR VERY BEST*

## *NAME: KARIN VOLO*

## About me

Born in Mexico to American and Swedish parents, I grew up in the US. I moved to Sweden with my young daughters when my first marriage ended. My biggest joy is my children and my wonderful second husband.

Professionally, I have 15 years experience with executive search and now specialize in personal development. I am passionate about helping people better their lives through mentoring, teaching, writing, and sharing all that I have learned on my journey.

After this major turning point, I founded www.InspiringYourVeryBest.com to help others through their tough transitions and create their own dream lives. I am also publishing a series of spiritual picture books that I wrote while incarcerated, explaining various spiritual concepts in a way that was easy for my children to understand − and helped them cope with our separation. The *Bringing Joy to...* series is the biggest gift from these tough times we experienced.

**Website:**  www.InspiringYourVeryBest.com
          www.KarinVolo.com
**Email:**    karin@InspiringYourVeryBest.com

**Gifts:**
As a way of showing my appreciation of you, I am offering three gifts. 1) a complimentary subscription to *Inspiring Lives* newsletter, 2) a free recording of my teleclass: *How to Stop the Downward Spiral and Start Living Your Dream Life*, and 3) the opportunity to apply for a Dream Life Discovery Session. Please go to www.InspiringYourVeryBest.com/gifts to claim these gifts.

# In the Beginning

[2]Everything seemed to be going beautifully for me; I had put behind me a disastrous first marriage to a con man and now had a wonderful, handsome business partner and fiancé named Sergio (from Spain), two delightful young daughters, two great bonus kids (Sergio's children) , and a successful executive recruiting business in Europe. We were working hard and growing our business, getting ready to expand in several countries and had finally just moved into our dream home. I had already come a long way in rebuilding my life and was so ready to take the next quantum leap. Little did I know that leap was going to be off a major cliff and down into the darkest, toughest time of my life.

One day in 2006, Sergio and I were at San Diego airport, waiting to catch a flight home after an empowering and energising week-long workshop with international business coach, John Assaraf, when I felt a tap on my shoulder. A U.S. Marshal said, "You have to come with me," and I spent the next three and three quarter years in jail, accused of things involving my first husband, before my case was dismissed and all charges cleared. In fact, by the end of this unbelievable odyssey, I had been jailed in a San Diego facility longer than any woman in its history.

I was very scared my life was in danger. As I fought extradition to Mexico, I knew it would be disastrous to give in to fear and despair. Back in Sweden, Sergio ran our business and took care of my daughters, and the two of us fought a rollercoaster legal battle involving two countries and several lawyers. Meanwhile, I had to find ways to stay positive. Sergio and I got married in a jailhouse ceremony, conducted in Swedish, under the noses of unsuspecting guards (a fellow inmate gifted me with a Snickers Bar wedding cake and a card written on a Tootsie Roll wrapper, a gesture I much appreciated). Armed with *Yoga for Dummies* from the prison library, I began leading yoga classes on the roof for my fellow inmates, and learned from them how to make tamales from warm water and crushed corn chips in a bag. I found strength as the other mothers and I encouraged each other to talk about our children and our hopes for them. I worked at turning fear into a solid belief that "today is the day I go home" even as I endured strip searches, sudden pat-downs and head counts, and separation from the man I love and my little girls for nearly four years. I had a 'book angel' friend who led me to writings that helped me claim my power to master my thoughts and beliefs. I was not going to let the uncertainty and deprivation cause me to become resentful or depressed, even though there were days when my fear and sadness threatened to overwhelm me.

I never stopped believing in the possibilities of what any of us can create for ourselves. My trust in the angels that surround us and support us is stronger now than ever. The way I see it, horrible as this nightmare was, it was an opportunity for me to do the deep soul-searching and growth that we all say we're going to get around to some day when we can find the time. Now I want to inspire others with my story of finding courage and hope.

[2]*This is a summary of my inspirational memoir, Wherever There Are Angels, I Am Safe, (due to be published 2012) which is based on my extraordinary experience.*

## My Turning Point

Looking back, those four years prepared me for what I consider now my life's purpose: to teach and inspire others to overcome challenges using their inner resources. I was given a gift of spiritual inspiration. I learned over time to focus each and every day on love – the love of my daughters and husband – so that I could be reunited with them. There is a saying that love is stronger than any other force. I know this to be true. If we stay focused on love, it makes life easier, it creates miracles, and it keeps everyone feeling better.

## Taking stock

At my Turning Point I knew my choices were…

- Fear, doubts, and uncertainty could easily have taken me over.
- When I learned to surrender completely, I was able to find peace.
- Trust has been a big issue with me because in my life, I've trusted the wrong people. I had to learn to trust in God because I had nothing else to rely on.
- Somehow I learned to tap into my inner resources. I got connected to my angels and this gave me strength.
- I refused to let go of my dream of being reunited with my family.
- I made a conscious choice every single day to focus on love and to not give into the darkness and fear – which I was surrounded by in my circumstances.

## Making it happen

I often get asked, how did you all manage? I honestly can say I don't really know now, except that I stayed focused on my dream. I knew enough about the law of attraction to know I had to keep myself in a positive state of mind (talk about a challenge in the environment I was in!) and I knew we create our lives with our thoughts. I learned a lot about forgiveness and appreciation. I learned how to pick myself up when I got knocked down, over and over again. I just wasn't going to let the legal or justice system 'beast' get me down. And I knew my determination to succeed would help me overcome all the negativity. I had an unwavering faith in my miracle – and it did come, finally. And what a sweet victory that was for me and my family!

## My plan for improvement

I...

- Searched for natural healing modalities to help improve and overcome the Post-Traumatic Stress Disorder (PTSD) symptoms I had to deal with and I've been amazed at how much is available now.
- Ate well to cleanse my body from four years of horrible processed foods.
- Exercised and continued with my yoga to maintain my health and keep in shape.
- Continued on my spiritual journey, but, with my energies now in the 'real' world, wanting to make a big impact to inspire and empower others.

## Moving forward my way

Because I want to make a positive difference in the world, I chose to work with inspiration. My story is inspirational because our love was so strong and our dream did come true. The cases were dismissed and I was reunited with my family. I've started a new business called Inspiring Your Very Best.

I teach others the tools and lessons I learned to overcome the biggest challenge in my life so that they too, can not only survive, but THRIVE, through any obstacles that life might put in our way. It truly IS possible to create your dream life!

## Wisdom from along the way

I have learned…

- Choose love, not fear.
- Focus on solutions, not the problems.
- "Your opinion of me is none of my business" – this saying from Wayne Dyer became one of my mantras in the midst of tremendous gossip and drama.
- Everyone is doing their best along their journey. Some are far behind and others are quite advanced on their spiritual journey.
- If a pattern repeats in your life, look for the lesson. Once you learn the lesson, you'll be able to move on.
- Forgiveness frees your heart. Practice forgiveness for yourself.

# Resources to rave about

## Books

*You Can Heal Your Life* Louise Hay (Hay House Inc, Carlsbad, CA, 1999 (1984))

*A Course in Miracles* New Christian Church of Full Endeavor, Ltd. (Wisconsin Dells, WI 2005)

*The 15 Minute Miracle Revealed* Jacquelyn Aldana (Inner Wisdom Publications, Los Gatos, CA, 2003)

*Conversations with God, Books 1, 2 & 3* Neale Donald Walsch (Hampton Roads Publishing Co, Charlottesville, NC, 1995, 1997, 1998)

*The Divine Matrix* Gregg Braden (Hay House Inc, Carlsbad, CA, 2007)

*Angel Medicine* by Doreen Virtue) Hay House Inc, Carlsbad, CA 2004)
 – I read seven books by Doreen Virtue and they taught me so much about connecting to our angels.

# FROM THE DEPTHS OF DESPERATE ADDICTION TO A NATURAL HIGH

## *ANNE'S STORY*
## *THREE LIVES IN ONE LIFETIME*

### *NAME: ANNE E PILLING*

## About me

I have learnt that there are no coincidences and everything works out for the best. Hence, it is no surprise I am writing my story 10 years to the day after moving my life from England to Nice, Cote d'Azur. As a five-year-old girl, I created a dream vision for myself and pursued it. Then, as I approached my 50th birthday in 2000, the vision changed. My direction may change again soon.

I am a Lancashire Lass and grew up with the single desire to be a nurse. Every birthday and Christmas, when asked what I would like for a gift, my answer was, "A nurse's set please." YOU were always my patient and I always helped you to get better, bandaged and nursed you with the highest level of care. But you had to do as you were told!

What a journey! How did it all happen?

**Website:** www.calmcarecounselling.com
**Email:** calmcare@orange.fr


## In the beginning

Home was not a very happy place for me as a child, and I moved into the nurses' home as soon as I could start working in hospitals, aged 16. I had the bare minimum of GCEs to begin my training, and I loved my work from day one. I attained four As for my hospital finals and passed my State Registration finals first time; my career had begun. The dream vision had started and nothing could stop me now!

I specialised in psychiatry, started my Registered Mental Nurse training in York, began a romance with a man and moved to work near him. I had a really strong desire to travel, to develop my career with a healthy income, confident of a roof over my head. Our relationship went on for four years until he demanded that I make a decision to either marry or join the Army and break off our engagement. I chose the Army!

I was a Captain in the Queen Alexandra's Royal Army Nursing Corps, on a two-year posting in Hong Kong, an extraordinary experience, full of fun, friends and fabulous adventures which revolved around cocktails in Kowloon and sticky liquors at Ned Kelly's Last Stand Bar.

I didn't notice my social life involved more alcohol than I could handle. My 'Doctor Prince' finished our relationship when I had my first withdrawal convulsion, prompting a five-year deterioration in my health. I hardly noticed my failing memory or my decision making being impaired. I thought everyone had hangovers and blackouts – the longer the blackout the better time I must have had! I was shocked when a very good-looking gentleman told me my life story, yet I didn't know him! I had been in a total blackout and couldn't even remember him.

There started to be consequences to my drinking and using other chemicals and pills. I had to resign my commission in the Army, and was suspended from duties in the next job. I was always very good at securing senior positions with great responsibility in prestigious hospitals, but by the third disciplinary action against me, I finally realized I needed help to stop drinking alcohol and to address my addictions, before I lost this job as well.

I listened, shook, and had no clue as to what would happen to me when I went to a rehabilitation centre. My director of nursing stated she wanted me back at work. Her trust in me was like a priceless jewel giving me a spark of life that had all but been extinguished. I had given up on myself, full of shame, disgust, self-pity, loneliness and a chronic self hatred. I thought there was something evil inside me that made me do these things, not realizing how very ill I was with the disease of addiction.

Two months of treatment helped me accept this illness that I hadn't asked for. I learnt I could recover one day at a time, as long as I developed my spiritual life, changing everything about me – another gift as I had come to loathe everything I stood for.

Within eight months I was head-hunted to go for training at Hazelden in the USA, the grandfather of alcohol rehabilitation centers and to join the team at a new centre in Kent. After 18 months there, and ready to develop my skills, I sent my CV around to all eight addiction centers in the UK. The internationally famous 'Farm Place' treatment facility employed me for the next 14 years.

## My Turning Point

My addictions – which my mother believed would be the end of me – heralded an amazing journey of self-discovery with an opportunity to help others recover from the depths of despair and addiction. However, sixteen years was enough in that specialty. I needed change.

I asked myself, "What haven't I done in my life?" I had never married nor run my own company. I had been salaried since 16, loved the human body and was developing my new spiritual path. As my 50th birthday approached, I wanted a simple life, to be warm, live by the sea and create my own company!

**Taking stock**

At my Turning Point I knew my choices were…

- I did not want to stay at Farm Place, as the treatment principles and people were all changing.

- I did not want to return to the health service; 20 years was all the nursing I intended to do. I was already a certified counsellor, wanting to offer something for the mind, body and spirit in a holistic approach to health and healing. I needed a name which epitomised what I wanted to offer to my clients and CalmCare was born.
- I knew one person who lived in Nice in the south of France. He suggested I should come to have a look. I came for one week in May 2000 and again in September, resulting in my decision to move to France!

## Making it happen

With the help of an agency, I rented my house in England, and asked for references from everyone whom I felt could be beneficial to me in France. Someone wanted to buy my car, but allowed me to use it until the last day in the UK.

My one and only friend in Nice offered me a place to stay. I didn't speak French, so I had to connect with the English speaking community. I took every opportunity to meet new people by going to English speaking places, gatherings and groups to introduce myself. The words 'networking' and 'marketing' were unknown to me, but another friend was a marketing consultant. I asked her and everyone else for help, keeping in close contact with my friends and family in England to give me support and encouragement.

# My plan for improvement

I...

- was gripped by Chronic FEAR. I needed to learn the language.
- studied Susan Jeffers' book, *Feel the Fear and Do It Anyway*, practising every tool.
- found a place to live and work, small and slightly dark, but in the best area of Nice.
- advertised in the local English language magazine and website and I got a list of    English speaking doctors and dentists.
- created cards and flyers in English. I made many mistakes, but it was all learning.
- resolved (and am still trying!) to make a friend of the computer – this machine which has been the bane of my life.
- knew I was on my own when my friend moved away. I needed an income and had to be pro-active and start to face communications in French.
- built on the one client from the UK I knew. Gradually, one by one, the community realised I was there. I offered a variety of services: massage, Reiki or counselling. As a Registered Nurse, my services as a nurse and companion were requested for six weeks, a live-in position which paid well and kept me afloat till after my first Christmas 2001.
- stayed fit with yoga, cycling along the promenade and reading many spiritual books to maintain my health and spiritual awareness.

- maintained connections with old colleagues and friends and returned to the UK once a year for training. My counselling supervisor and I spoke twice a month.
- practised my faith that 'all would be well' in 2006 when my bike and I were hit by a car, breaking my left hip and arm. Three months in a wheelchair cured my financial insecurity. My prudent reserve kept me afloat as there was no income. All was well, and my French improved too!

## Moving forward my way

I have been involved with many groups and gatherings to bring people together. My fears turned into a new business as I became a trainer with Susan Jeffers – facilitating workshops based on her book, *Feel the Fear and Do It Anyway*.

As a result of our work, some people have found their recovery programme. I have been a channel, and a useful member of our community. A new vision is coming through – Belize is calling. Next month I'll visit this country to look at retiring there. Belize is English speaking with English law – phew, no more French!

## Wisdom from along the way

I have learned…

- Let go of the FEAR (False Evidence Appearing Real). It's an illusion.

- YOU are the only person in charge of your thinking. Thoughts become things; chose the GOOD ones.
- Always come from a place of love. What you give out you will get back, by the Law of Attraction.
- Life unfolds as it is meant to. Go with the flow, and trust the Universe.
- Don't blame anyone for how you feel, where you are or what you are doing. Your decisions put you where you are. Check them carefully before all major changes.
- Create your own positive future; don't give up, keep breathing and moving forward.
- Keep the focus on generating income.
- Everything is possible; give 100 per cent attention to your dream vision; believe in yourself.
- Know your competition, but don't worry about it.
- Play and have fun time. Make a point of creating interests, hobbies and healthy habits.

## Resources to rave about

### Books

*Feel the Fear and Do it Anyway* Susan Jeffers (Rider, 1991)

*You Can Heal Your Life* Louise Hay (Hay House)
*Change Your Thoughts, Change Your Life* Dr Wayne Dyer (Hay House)

*Conversations with God* Neale Donald Walsch (Hodder and Stoughton)

# FROM SHREDDED PROSPECTS TO FREEDOM

## *BETH'S STORY*
## *FINDING MY PASSION*

## *NAME: BETH HOBAN*

## About me

Dynamic, supportive, creative, resourceful and dedicated is how my clients describe me. Having designed my own portable career and business that compliments a global lifestyle, I use my 14+ years of experience in human resources, coaching, and training to help clients develop and enhance their international careers. I am a certified career coach and business skills trainer specializing in expatriate transition and cross-cultural training.

My clients have launched their own international businesses, served in senior diplomatic posts, successfully returned to the workforce after taking time off to raise a family and worked in fortune 500 companies and top consulting firms.

I am an American who has lived in Germany, Korea, the Philippines and is currently residing in Saudi Arabia. I am the proud wife of a US diplomat and mom to three Third Culture Kids (children who have grown up in countries that are not the passport country of either parent) all born in different countries.

**Website:**   www.expattransitions.com
**Email:**   beth@expattransitions.com

**Gifts:** Complimentary one-hour coaching session or resume review. Invitation to beta test new e-courses. To access these, send me an email and include the words "turning points" in the subject line.

## In the beginning

It was an unusually warm October day. I took a subtle glance at my watch as I felt the afternoon slump set in. It was 2:30 and I was conducting my sixth interview of the day in the small, stuffy interview room at the University of Texas MBA School. I sat in my stylish, yet professional, black pants-suit and pearls across from the eager business student outfitted in his new pinstripe suit, crisp white dress shirt and, of course, red power tie. The interview was wrapping up and I asked, "Do you have any questions?"

"Can you give me an update on the relationship between Enron and your firm?" the recruit asked.

"Enron. Oh, I'm sure that matter will be resolved shortly," I said smugly as I wrapped up the interview and told him that we would be in touch.

Truthfully speaking, I was not 100 per cent sure what the recruit was talking about. I knew Enron was a large energy company and a top client. I had heard faint rumors about an accounting scandal, but I didn't know much else. Little did I know at that time the impact Enron would have on my career.

Six months later, the whole world had heard of Enron. Enron and my firm were embroiled in an accounting scandal that rocked the global business community and would soon become synonymous with shredded documents, cover-ups and ethical violations.

One quiet April morning, my boss called me to his office.

"Elizabeth, our team is being let go."

I was in shock that the layoffs happened so quickly. In three months, 26,000 employees in the United States were laid off or sold to other practices. All along I had genuinely believed the firm would pull through.

Large tears filled my eyes and fear filled my heart. What would I do? We had just bought our first house with a decent sized mortgage. I had been accepted on a PhD program that my company benefits would pay for. I was up for promotion to manager. My perfect plans crumbled. Now what?

I did what any logical and responsible person would do – looked for a similar position at another firm. A few weeks later, I landed a good job. Actually, on paper it was a better job – promotion, more money, additional responsibility, and less travel. Maybe getting laid off was a blessing. I would finally have the time I had been looking for.

On the surface, all the pieces appeared to fit – good job, happy marriage, great social life, even time to train for a marathon. What more could I ask?

Yet, I was miserable. In a job I hated, I woke every morning dreading going to work. I tried to shake it off and blamed it on missing my previous co-workers. I rationalized that I wasn't really giving the job a fair chance, I would snap out of it. As time passed, I realized I was drowning in work I didn't enjoy and couldn't get my head above water. I soon learned I was pregnant. I felt like I was trapped in a bad situation and couldn't find my way out of this confining cubicle. Not in a position to change jobs because I needed health insurance and maternity leave, I decided I would do the noble, martyr thing and sacrifice my passion and happiness for stability.

I miserably worked up until the day my son was born. On maternity leave it was such a blessing to have time to gather my thoughts, but as my two-month leave came to an end I dreaded returning to work.

## My Turning Point

About three miserable weeks after returning to work, my husband called home on a Friday afternoon at 6pm. He said, "You know the overseas assignment I was offered next year? Well they want me to come early."

"Okay, so how early?" I asked.

"If you say yes right now the movers will be here on Monday," he said.

Wow!!! 48 hours to prepare for an international move. Give up my home, family, friends, career and move to Korea. I must be crazy!

I called my boss a half an hour later and gave my notice. I was finally free. But free to do what?

---

## Taking stock

At my Turning Point I knew my choices were…

- I could give up my career and be a stay-at-home mom. Money was no longer the primary driving factor.
- I could look for full-time or part-time positions in international companies.
- I could reconnect with my passion for helping people.
- I could be my own boss and set my own hours and choose my own projects and clients.

---

## Making it happen

I joined my husband in Korea, relishing the opportunity to settle into our new home and spend time with our son. About a week into my new position as stay-at-home mom, I realized I needed more. I loved being with my son, but in my heart knew I would be a better wife, mom and person if I was connected with my passion.

I knew I loved training and coaching people. I got so excited helping people shape their career or solve a problem at work. I wanted to lead training classes and use my knowledge to benefit others. Would it be possible to do this on my own? I knew I was talented. I started to explore all possibilities, began building my professional network and demonstrating the value I could add to any organization. I determined to work, but still be in control of my schedule and working hours.

## My plan for improvement

I...

- analyzed my previous positions and got clear on what worked and didn't work for me.
- established a needs and wants list, then prioritized the list.
- developed my personal brand – I needed to determine what set me apart from others.
- expanded my training and professional development – enrolled in advanced coaching courses with Coach U and DOOR international.
- joined professional associations –Human Resources, training and coaching groups.
- created a networking plan – made a target list of people and company representatives I wanted to meet.
- developed a business marketing plan to promote my services.

## Moving forward my way

I identified a number of organizational contacts in career coaching, training and consulting. Through networking I met clients interested in individual career coaching; these connections led me to a job as a radio co-host for a program targeting expats in Korea.

It has taken a number of years to grow my business, and it continues to be a learning process each day; every six months I revisit my action plans and goals and adjust as necessary. As I have moved from country to country, I have adapted my business skills to meet the needs of the community where I am living.

## Wisdom from along the way

I have learned…

- If you don't like something, change it. If you can't change it, you can still change the way you feel about it.
- Don't let perfection be the enemy of the good. Sometimes good is good enough.
- Constantly work on growing your network. Don't wait until you need a network to try and build it.
- Don't let the fear of failure keep you from trying something new.
- Hire help when you need it. Get a coach, accountant, lawyer, web designer or whatever you need so you can get back to doing the work you love.
- Pay it forward! Help others when you can and you will be rewarded in the future.

- Find mentors. I have many mentors, each with a different skill set that I seek guidance on.
- Join a women's networking group. If there isn't one near you, start one.

## Resources to rave about

**Books**
*The Power of Story* Jim Loehr (Free Press Reprint, 2008)

**Web**
Mind mapping is an excellent brainstorming tool, www.mindtools.com/pages/article/newISS_01.htm

For a brief overview visit http://www.mindtools.com/pages/article/newISS_01.htm

**Organisations**
Toastmasters International, find a group near you at www.Toastmasters.org, a group devoted to improving communication and leadership skills.

Coach University, www.CoachUniversity.com, excellent coaching programs

# FROM UNWORTHINESS TO WORTH

*FREDERIQUE'S STORY*
*THE JOURNEY TO EMPOWERING OTHERS TO*
*DO THE SAME.*

*NAME: FREDERIQUE MURPHY*

## About me

The reason why I smile all the time, is that I LOVE what I do ;-) I live fully on purpose. Half Irish, half French, and married to Roland, a Dutch man (love the nationality mix), I live in Ireland and fly around the world, to fulfil my mission.

My business is the platform to my dreams to passionately inspire, guide, and empower people, all over the world, to access their full potential, live their life to the fullest and always be true to themselves. Combining business expertise with mind expertise, I have developed the 'Mountain Moving Mindset' programme, where I empower business owners and entrepreneurs to master their mindset, thus, producing more results and boosting profits. You see, I believe that a strong mindset gives you the power to move mountains and the power to take your life and your business to a whole new level!

**Website:** www.frederiquemurphy.com
**Email:** connect@frederiquemurphy.com

**Gift:** *M.I.N.D.S.E.T., Your 7-Day Business Transformation Roadmap* Follow these seven key business strategies and within a week you will have built your own Transformation Roadmap! Available from my website: www.frederiquemurphy.com.

## In the beginning

My brother Fabien is gone. Sébastien left home three years ago, since when we have only seen him a couple of times. Now Fabien has left too.

Standing in the kitchen, chills down my spine, I read the papers Maman has received from the court, sent by my brothers' father, to terminate her parental rights. I'm 18 and it has been a very difficult couple of years; the atmosphere at home has been awful: repeated clashes between Maman, her partner, and us, my brothers and me.

So much pain, anger, sadness and hurt. I am upset; this pile of papers is simply crushing, and my hands are shaking. Harsh words are being used and as I stand there,

I feel immensely alone and stuck in between, thinking of Maman on one side and my brothers on the other, and how they must be feeling. It all comes down to these legal papers now in my shaking hands.

From the court's point of view, Sébastien, 15, Fabien, 14, and Loïc, 12, are my *half* brothers, but to me they have always been my brothers, full stop. No difference to me, it is not about blood, but heart; as the eldest, I was there for each of their births and ever since, so proud of being their *grande soeur*.

Except now, it hits me... This is not going to be possible anymore, as half siblings do not get visitation rights and my name is not mentioned anywhere. Unable to move, my mind racing, I struggle to cope with the realisation that this is it; Sébastien and Fabien are gone. Spending our childhood together seems not to matter anymore.

Tears running down my face, I turned to Maman, and said, "*C'est comme ci je n'existe pas...* " It was like I didn't exist. That was the moment when my heart shattered into thousands of pieces – I was heart-broken.

I was in the last year of school, called *Terminale*, and the *baccalauréat* exam was in a couple of months. I was struggling, studying so hard but just about reaching average. My quarterly grade reports said: "*Beaucoup de bonne volonté, continuez vos efforts.*» It was just not good enough, and that is how I felt: like I was not good enough. I felt like a failure.

After countless, sleepless nights of study, the exam date arrived. The pressure to succeed was immense; having the *bac* meant being able to pursue university studies, and that was what was expected.

A few weeks later, Maman and I drove back to school where the results had been posted. There were so many people in front of the school doors: some laughing, some crying, some hugging; it was very noisy. But, in that moment, as I walked across the crowd and looked for the M list and my surname, Murphy, everything became silent. Years of education, work and effort all brought me to this list, where my future would be announced by one word. I crossed my fingers, hoping for the word "*Admis*" next to my name. And, it was. But it was not a victory; another queue later I got my actual grades and, yes, I had passed, but barely. I was sick to my stomach; these grades did not match the level of work and effort I had put in.

So again I had failed: failed in my studies just as I had failed at home, feeling it was my fault, and that I should have been able to do something about the whole situation, to ensure we would all stay together. But no, I had failed; my brothers had left.


## My Turning Point

Having *barely* passed the exam, options were limited. As I did not know what I wanted to do, it seemed best to follow what was expected and register for a year at university.

And, then, another blow: Loïc announced he was leaving too. I had lost all my brothers. I had never felt *that* lonely before; they were all gone. That was too much: I was lost, felt abandoned; I did not know what I wanted to do after school, I didn't even truly know who I was.

I knew, however, it was time to do something – something had to change.

## Taking stock

At my Turning Point I knew my choices were...

- I could have stayed in the house, in that lonely house, and spent my summer crying.
- I could have settled and followed the conventional after-school university path.
- I could have accepted that my only school option was to study a topic I was not that interested in, nor passionate about, because it was the standard thing to do.
- Or, I could decide that this was the time to live my life, believe in me, believe I deserve, and make it work.

## Making it happen

I made the important decision to go away for the summer and got a two-month contract with an American company, Gateway Computers, based in Dublin. Within four days of the idea, flights and bed and breakfast were booked, and I was on the plane, with a 50lb suitcase, a smile on my face and full of faith. Having made the decision, I was committed to making it work. Landing in Dublin, the AerLingus stewardess welcomed us in English; the only word I understood was "Dublin".

As a child, my grandfather had proudly talked to me about being a real Murphy and Ireland felt like home from the very first day I arrived.

So I started a self-discovery journey. I felt free, and went from feeling shy, withdrawn, and awkward to being empowered to be the true me. It was important to find myself first, knowing that my purpose would follow.

# My plan for improvement

I...

- read self-development books, and invested in self-development training programmes –
- delivered outstanding work at all times, which got me noticed and, in time, a permanent job offer.
- improved my English – English has now become my first language; it is the language I use to think, make lists, dream, and work.
- became an Irish citizen; born a Murphy, I am an Irish woman at heart so it felt very natural to officialise the identity.
- discovered what I love doing: empowering people to make their dreams come true.
- learned, trained and became internationally recognised and licensed with various mind components, such as Neuro-Linguistic Programming, Ericksonian Hypnosis, Neurological Repatterning, and more.
- obtained a series of degrees in communications, marketing, design, and advertising through evening classes and distance learning organisations to back up my work experiences with qualifications.
- held various jobs and positions, building up my mind and business expertise, working as a communications and change management consultant on multi-million programmes around the world.

## Moving forward my way

Before reaching 30 I launched my own business, built on my two passions: mind and business. I LOVE what I do, and my business enables me to live my dream life with my husband, Roland, whose love and support have made a BIG contribution to my success, and also to make a difference in the world – what I call *true* wealth.

On September 30th, the phone rang; after six years of *complete* silence, I heard my brothers' voices, wishing me happy birthday. I stood, speechless and trembling. That was *the* phone call of the decade!

## Wisdom from along the way

I have learned...

- Everything happens for a reason and sometimes we are not able to understand why, but our past life experiences and events shape us into the people we are today.
- People do the best they can with the resources they have available at the time.
- Believe in your uniqueness and individuality, in your business, and in your dreams; identify the beliefs that do not serve you and create new powerful ones.
- When you master your mindset, you free yourself to achieve the level of business success you desire and deserve - the key to your business success is you, and you are 100 per cent responsible for your results and success.
- In life and business, when an opportunity comes along there is no point waiting, make the decision, jump in

and move forward. Without the decision, there is no action; without action, there are no results; and without results, there is no success.

- Be determined. Be focused. Be aligned and congruent. Persevere until you succeed.
- Surround yourself with a network of excellence - coaches, mentors, trainers, experts, and friends - it takes a team to make truly big things happen.
- Be 100 per cent connected with your vision, your big why, and your purpose; it is this that gives you the consistent and continuous drive to accomplish your business goals.
- Consistently invest your time, energy and money to model the best, and financial results will follow.
- You can achieve anything you set your mind to.

## Resources to rave about

**Books**
*Awaken the Giant Within* Anthony Robbins (Simon & Schuster, New York, 1992)

**People**
Amy Brann, www.synapticpotential.com, an empowering and very gifted coach, who has been key to my own personal journey.

**Organisations**
The Irish Institute of NLP, www.nlp.ie, co-founded by Owen Fitzpatrick and Brian Colbert, where I was taught my first NLP course.

# FROM SELF DOUBT TO SELF ESTEEM

*TRACY'S STORY*
*A WORLD THAT HAD BEEN FULL OF FEAR,*
*INSECURITY AND UNWORTHINESS WOULD NO*
*LONGER TAKE UP SPACE IN MY LIFE.*

*NAME: TRACY NEELY CNHP CHHC*

## About me

Tracy is an internationally recognized Holistic Nutrition Coach and Skin Health Expert who specializes in helping people make the move to go gluten, dairy, soy and sugar free. In her work, Tracy incorporates a holistic approach to heal the body, increase energy, and achieve optimum health, beauty, and balance in life naturally.

Whether it's clearing up your skin or cleansing toxins from your body, Tracy shows her clients how to optimize health, increase vibrancy and truly feel beautiful from the inside out. Tracy's motto is 'Beauty and Health Go Hand in Hand'. Tracy lives in Alpharetta, Georgia, with her husband and young son.

**Website:** www.NourishandFlourishHealthyLiving.com
**Email:** Tracy@NourishandFlourishHealthyLiving.com

**Gifts:** 30-minute Beauty Transformation Breakthrough Session, 10 Simple Tips to Healthy Radiant Skin, and Tracy's Health and Beauty E-Newsletter subscription loaded with insider tips and articles on beauty, health, skin care, nutrition, delicious recipes and support for living a healthy, vibrant life!
All available from my website:
www.NourishandFlourishHealthyLiving.com

## In the beginning

In 1988, at the age of 23, I was living in my hometown, Chattanooga, Tennessee, but had always dreamed of living in New York City; it represented an exciting life with endless opportunities. I knew some day it would be my reality. One day I asked my father if he had any contacts there. He made a call and soon I was on a plane to interview with a company in the fashion industry.

I'll never forget flying into LaGuardia Airport with butterflies in my stomach. After interviewing with a very nice gentleman, I was asked, "So when can you start?" ..

"Immediately!" I replied. I couldn't believe I was getting a chance to live my dream.

On April 30th 1988 I left my hometown to start a new life in the big city. Over the next two years, I came to love the excitement of living in a city that never sleeps. I wanted to explore everything New York offered. I lived in a tiny one-room apartment in the heart of the city on East 22nd Street. I thought: *this is the life: a doorman apartment, a job I love and the life I always dreamed of.*

On a visit home to my mom, I decided to have a routine dental check-up. Since I hadn't visited the dentist in a while, he took an X-ray to check if everything was fine. What showed up was a black spot and a strange look came over his face.

"Is everything okay?" I asked. He said I should see an oral surgeon for further tests.

I was convinced that there had been a glitch, but after getting the news that it looked like I had a very rare tumor in my lower jaw, I was literally numb.

With all kinds of thoughts swirling in my mind, all I remember saying is, "I'm leaving for New York tomorrow."

It took a while to process the news I'd been given and I wondered how to tell my parents. After assuring my mom that everything would be fine, I returned to New York. My mind was racing. How could I possibly have a tumor? And where had it come from?

Two weeks later, I was sitting in front of yet another oral surgeon. I had a very rare tumor called ameloblastoma that was growing at an accelerated rate.

"We have to do surgery tomorrow. If we don't remove this tumor, it will spread to your upper jaw, then to your brain and it will be inoperable."

I thought I was going to faint. As I sat watching the dentist's mouth move, my mind was far away. It was like he was speaking through water. He mentioned they would need to remove four teeth around the tumor and after the surgery we would talk about dental implants, and so on.

That night I called my parents and gave them the news. The next day, after enduring a five-hour surgery, I was told the tumor was bigger than they had thought and they had removed all but two of my bottom teeth. All I kept thinking was: how would I ever date again?

As I was wheeled into recovery, I felt my jaw which was covered in heavy bandages. Even though I was in excruciating pain, I was fixated on my face. What did I look like? How bad was it? A nurse smiled gently as she handed me a mirror. What I saw frightened me. My entire head was wrapped in bandages to support my jaw. My face was swollen to the size of a basketball and my lips swollen like two hot dogs. I wanted to scream.

## My Turning Point

After leaving the hospital, I stayed at the Flatotel in New York. Waiting for my mother to join me there and help me recover, I really wanted to look my best, so I combed my hair and found a tube of bright red lipstick in the bottom of my purse. However, despite my best efforts, I looked nothing like my old self. When my mother walked in, her eyes teared up and though she tried, she could barely meet my eyes. Although all I really wanted to do was cry, I put up a good face and smiled the best I could.

## Taking stock

At my Turning Point I knew my choices were…

- I could have a pity party and ask myself, "Why me?" and be angry at the world.
- I could just simply spend the rest of my life hiding, too embarrassed by my looks.
- I could decide my life would never amount to anything special since something so horrific had happened to me.
- Or, I could see the blessing in my decision to have a routine dental visit and do everything in my power to heal my body and honor my fierce determination that I would turn my life around.

## Making it happen

My motto has always been 'beauty from the inside out,' and once my body started healing, I decided that it was time to start walking my talk. Instead of spending my time staring at the mirror and lamenting what might have been, I started working on improving my mind and my spirit by praying more, doing meditation, and I started doing yoga. I began to truly appreciate that I was on an ongoing journey of discovery that could lead to me living better, finding beauty in all things, being healthier, and striving for wholeness. The surgery wasn't the end; it was the beginning and soon I was determined to live a truly holistic life.

# My plan for improvement

I...

- knew that supporting others in their quest to live a healthy, vibrant life was something I wanted to pursue as a career.
- explored what I was passionate about and realized that I had always loved everything about skin care, beauty and nutrition.
- decided to go back to school to become licensed as an esthetician (skin care therapist) and graduated with a B.S. degree in Holistic Nutrition from Clayton College of Natural Health.
- decided to take my passion and turn it into a business, Nourish & Flourish Healthy Living.
- began studying marketing and sales to determine ways to create residual and passive income:
- worked with a business coach to learn every aspect of marketing and supporting my clients long term.
- wrote my first ebook, a monthly e-newsletter and an online program '10 Days to Healthy Radiant Skin', allowing me to reach even more clients and to earn the passive income to spend more time with my husband and son.
- created to connect with current and potential clients.
- teamed up with local practitioners in my area and created cutting edge 'Lunch and Learn' seminars to take my message to the next level.
- invested in training programs that would give me the tools to learn every aspect of growing my business.

- took the time to develop my own health and wellness routine which included a daily practice of yoga, meditation, aromatherapy, exercise, juicing and cooking.

## Moving forward my way

Looking back at a time full of sadness, anger and yes, self-pity, I now embrace everything that happened including the re-constructive surgery where bone marrow from my hip was placed in my jaw. And although the shape of my face has changed, I now realize that my inner beauty was always there. More importantly, because of those traumas, I am committed to living with joy, love, and purpose and helping my clients, no matter what their condition, do the same.

I now have a thriving health and wellness practice, and, as I move into the next phase of life and business, I am grateful for the opportunity to support women. My motto of 'Beauty and Health Go Hand in Hand' has never been more relevant.

## Wisdom from along the way

I have learned…

- Wealth is not just measured in dollars; a healthy body, mind and spirit are your greatest assets.
- Beauty is not just your appearance; it's your state of mind.

- Gratitude is one of our best gifts.
- Laughter can bring you through any situation.
- Your past does not have to continue to keep you in a state of flux.
- Continuing to educate yourself in your field will give you the tools to stay on top of your game.
- Adversity creates opportunities along the way.
- Every day may not be what you planned for, but find something good in every day.
- Change has been a constant in my life that has allowed me to grow.

## Resources to rave about

### Books

*Excuse Me Your Life Is Waiting: The Astonishing Power of Feelings* Lynn Grabhorn (Hampton Roads Publishing; 1st Trade Paper edition, 2003)

*Money, and the Law of Attraction: Learning to Attract Wealth, Health, and Happiness* Esther Hicks and Jerry Hicks (Hay House, 2008)

*The Big Leap: Conquer Your Hidden Fear and Take Life to the Next Level* Gay Hendricks (HarperOne, 2010)

*The Costly Anointing* Lori Wilke
(Destiny Image Publishers, 1992)

# FROM HELPLESSNESS TO INDEPENDENCE

## *ALEKSANDRA'S STORY*
## *IT TAKES A TURNING POINT TO START THE JOURNEY OF SELF-DISCOVERY*

## *NAME: ALEKSANDRA TURNER*

## About me

I am motivated by a self-felt calling to the cause of good, growth, and gain in the lives of others. I can be called on when a fresh, new way to communicate important information is needed, and in situations where I can express new ideas, key concepts or plots. I look for opportunity, challenge, and risk – I thrive on change, and know how to capitalize on it.

I will automatically and naturally see the links, relationships and patterns between different ideas – 'the big picture'. I can be a big help with strategic planning and identifying possibilities.

I am very proud of my son, with whom I live in London, where I also give my time to work in support of local issues.

**Email:**     aleksandravojvodic@tiscali.co.uk

**Gift:** Email me your contact details to arrange a FREE one-hour telephone session if you would like me to think through some new ideas with you, explore different ways of moving forward, or find a new focus to aid and refresh your strategy. I will then call you back.

## In the beginning

A very turbulent evening was followed by a dark, quiet night. As I recovered consciousness and got up off the living room floor, I slowly and carefully gathered my sleeping two-year-old son and a few necessary items and fled into the night, my heart and my mind racing each other. I had nowhere to go, but my legs kept on moving faster and faster – I had to get as far away as possible from my (then) home and (now ex) husband, as I feared for my son's safety and my own life. About a mile away I entered the empty shopping centre. It looked sad and deserted without the jostle, chat and laughter of shoppers that enliven it throughout the day.

Alone, scared and helpless, I sat on the bench, holding my son, thinking about what to do. Suddenly, I remembered my friend and former neighbour to whom I felt close at that time. Living as a housewife next door, I enjoyed helping Jean by doing her shopping, cleaning, ironing, gardening and painting. I had never found it easy to ask for help, but having no other choice I made my way to her house and knocked on the door. I felt lucky and shielded as the front door closed behind me and the warmth and safety of the surroundings enveloped us.

Jean knew about my threatening situation at home and allowed me to stay with her until I could collect myself and re-organise my life. All the members of my family live across several European countries, and I had no one here in London, so I was extremely grateful for her kindness. I still felt dazed, confused, with the sensation of being outside my own body, and not fully aware of where I was going and what I should do. I kept looking over my shoulder wherever I walked, living in constant fear, believing he was going to come after me.

"I am sorry but you cannot stay here any longer – I have visitors arriving in three days and need more space to accommodate them. You'll need to find somewhere else to stay," said Jean, quite coldly and directly. I stood on her doorstep on that sunny, warm summer afternoon, and felt struck by those words – less than a week after I had arrived with my tiny son, seeking shelter, support and escape from pain. Just as I slowly started hoping that I was crawling out of the hole my life had become over the past five years, I felt those words tip me back over the edge into the abyss of uncertainty and fear.

As I stood on that doorstep, I was unable to move, neither to go in nor to back out, looking on, bewildered and unbelieving, at the future of homelessness.

## My Turning Point

I was ashamed of my own bad choice of husband and too proud to admit my failure. I preferred silence to sharing complaints about my life with my family – I always felt that they, being far away and unable to help, particularly my mum who suffers with MS, did not need to hear anything negative or worrisome about me.

Although I could not clearly envision the future in the state I was in that sunny afternoon, I somehow knew that I had to keep striving, keep going, keep looking for solutions. I had turned a corner and I wasn't going back.

### Taking stock

At my Turning Point I knew my choices were…

- I could sink deeper into myself and resign myself to whatever life would throw at me in the future.
- I could sit on the street and hope that help would somehow materialise out of nowhere.
- I could go out into the world, face the challenge and actively seek help to change my situation as well as myself and ensure a happier future for my son.

## Making it happen

Although I had felt alone, I found that I had some true friends. I had been doing a lot of voluntary work over several years for an organisation whose members were worried after failing to see me for some time. After contacting them for advice, I ended up with all the help I could wish for, housing for us both, free babysitting services and a solicitor who was able to procure an injunction against my husband in one day. Proceedings were started immediately, which in due course meant that I was able to move back into my home with my son.

The rest was down to me as I followed my heartfelt ethics of hard work, perseverance and determination not only to provide a loving home atmosphere and role model for my son but also to succeed professionally and facilitate others' success.

## My plan for improvement

With my broad aims to guide me, I...

- read a lot of women's literature of all kinds which let me see that a different future was possible and gave me confidence to further develop myself.
- read widely on and consulted others about child development and childcare.
- completed the BSc (Hons) while working as a silver service waitress at banks, hotels, race-courses, conferences, banquets...
- obtained a job as a hotel manager – I enjoyed growing the business and having the freedom to shape all the

activity in the hotel and restaurant, while completing an MA at the same time.

- moved on to manage a reputable high-end restaurant, continuously attending courses to aid my professional development.
- got to know myself better – my inquisitive, exploratory, analytical, and experimental nature meant I needed to constantly challenge myself with creative or innovative activities in order to stay happy and productive, both professionally and in my private life.
- entered the world of contract catering. It made sense to work office hours when my son started high school. I now manage accounts and sites in London and Edinburgh and am currently halfway through my MBA studies.
- worked on structuring my responsibilities with the aim of gaining more time for giving, as well as for contemplation and freethinking.
- have been continuously working on my goal to facilitate the success of others over the years by mentoring and helping them to achieve their aims no matter how far-fetched they might seem at the start.

## Moving forward my way

'Forward' is the word that rightly describes my outlook on life – I am happy in the present and am always looking to the future with relish and in anticipation of challenges to come – the past is now only a distant reminder of how loss of independence can slowly erode the sense of self-confidence and self-belief that is so essential for success in all areas of life. My way forward includes the promise to never lose my hard-won independence again and to continually support other women who are struggling or striving towards it. It takes a Turning Point to start the journey of self-discovery and create a vision of the future that allows for a life rich in freedom and independence.

## Wisdom from along the way

I have learned…

- Happiness is within us – so resist others' (even loved ones') expectations and ideas of who you should be – listen to your own mind and intuition – it will allow you to grow, develop and become exactly the kind of person you like and respect. Success in all areas of life depends on it and stems from it.
- If that does not come easy, then simply enlist help – some of the other contributors in this book, such as Kate Cobb, can coach you towards achieving your goals.
- My way is not straying from this simple principle: always give more than you take – this can be challenging at times as I am continually overjoyed by life's opportunities and at times surprised at its generosity!
- Yes, it is true – sometimes you need to close that one door and turn around to see the other three doors that are wide open and waiting for you.

# Resources to rave about

## Books
*How Women Mean Business: A Step by Step Guide to Profiting from Gender Balanced Business* A. Wittenberg-Cox (John Wiley and Sons Ltd, Chichester, 2010)

*Fierce Leadership: A Bold Alternative to the Worst 'Best' Practices of Business Today* Susan Scott (Crown Business Publishing, Random House, New York, 2009)

*Ideas with Impact: HBR on Women in Business* (Harvard Business School Press, Boston, 2005)

*Infidel* Ayaan Hirsi Ali (Simon and Schuster, New York, 2007). Ayaan is extremely brave and, I believe, the most inspiring woman

## Web
MindTools.com, www.mindtools.com, excellent resource for leadership training and management techniques

MAPP Assessment, www.assessment.com/, I have done many career assessment tests, but this is the best to help you grow

# FROM PAIN, GRIEF AND LOSS TO FREEDOM

## *JANET'S STORY*
## *FINDING AND WALKING THE RAINBOW BRIDGE*

### *NAME: JANET ORION*

## About me

I am a natural medicine woman, a sort of fairy godmother, health intuitive, change agent and spiritual mentor for cultural creatives on the verge of greatness. For most of us, dramatic changes feel like labor and delivery without any preparation or support. With all the amazing tools for transformation available – some so simple we might overlook them – we shift all that seeming drama into the miraculous.

I take people on inner journeys through the power of breathing, exploring, inquiring: finding real solutions to life's challenges. We explore simple keys to freedom, health, happiness and trust. The muscle-testing I learned decades ago and the dowsing I teach my clients help us zero-in on what's really happening and make the best choices as we navigate life's circumstances. I coach people via Skype to find the God-Source within, leave pain and access the gain that is available. I'm living in Los Angeles for the second time after living in lots of great places. I have no children, am single and available for a soulmate relationship.

**Website:** http://JanetOrion.org
**Email:** getDrJanet@msn.com

**Gifts:** Visit my website http://JanetOrion.org and click on the tab 'Healthy Ways' at the top. As you scroll down the page you will see the Wheel of Life exercise. Do the exercise and send me an email about your discoveries. I will gift one person a week with a 30-minute session with me via Skype video which we will arrange to suit our schedules so we can get acquainted, explore and look at resources and possibilities that help you move forward in any area of your life.

## In the beginning

Many events in my life have caused me to wake up, pay attention, and make life-altering choices. I actually had a very happy, loving, safe childhood. The only blight on my early years was the impact of World War II. My father was a captain in Patton's Third Army, on the front lines in Europe in 1944-1945. I can only imagine what his life was like in that heinous chapter in planetary history. Dad never talked about the war. But its traumas took their toll, on him, on my family, and on me.

The happy childhood was totally over by the time I was 15. We moved from my hometown, my friends, as I entered the 11th grade. Maybe it was because I was pretty or because I didn't know how important designer labels and the right status symbols were, but I was shunned by the girls and the boys were hesitant to befriend me, because they were locked into relationships. I was lonely and miserable in our new home. I didn't belong. I was on my own.

Then, to make matters much worse, my mother found a lump in her breast. In 1965, the medical solution was a truly radical mastectomy. Life was no longer safe. I saw my dad cry for the first time, as we watched my mother lying in her hospital bed looking very gray and scary. Cancer in those days meant death. And no one ever said the word 'breast' except when they whispered "breast cancer". My seven-year-old brother threw up in the hallway outside Mom's hospital room. I had the direct experience of 'Paradise Lost'.

To further shatter any illusion of a support system in my community, we moved again the next summer. No one in my family ever questioned my dad's choices.

This time we moved to another new city. What was my dad thinking? What were *we* thinking to go along for this chaotic ride of his, searching for something he didn't talk about? Maybe I just didn't care any more if I had friends or not, but this year seemed easier than the last year. Until my dad had a health scare one night. When he returned from the hospital the next day, either the doctors couldn't find what was wrong with him, or he didn't want us to know. He started eating healthier and lost 30 pounds he probably hated and then put a bullet through his head the summer I graduated high school. That day everything changed.

## My Turning Point

I vowed that day to learn about health, life, God, and truth. I woke up fast. For that I'm grateful. The pain was enormous.

I've faced many other 'Turning Points': wild wasteful college years, abortion, the death of the love of my life, gaining 30 pounds of 'armor'. I did a 55-day water fast that almost killed me. I was kidnapped and raped on Kauai. I joined a 'spiritual community' that was awesome and abusive. I had years of chronic severe back pain. I lost everything and started over several times. Each event compounded the shock of my father's suicide and contributed to my next step in 1985 when I went back to school.

## Taking stock

At my Turning Point I knew my choices were…

- Give up and ruin my life.
- Stay in the situation and in the dark.
- Get my own health situation sorted out.
- Take practical steps to pursue my interest in the natural healing arts.
- Realize that I am 30 years ahead of most in understanding and in my awareness of conditions on earth.

## Making it happen

I decided to go to chiropractic school, accruing massive debt, because I had a burning desire to help people be healthy. My back attacks continued. People tried, but nothing seemed to help me. It wasn't until 1988 when I met a chiropractor who did this amazing type of muscle response testing (kinesiology) with 'hand modes' that I finally got help with my health problems.

He discovered that I had a beef tapeworm. I accepted that. After all, the three cows that lived in Kalalau Valley shared mangoes and the stream for drinking water with my boyfriend and me. Muscle-testing identified my need for a nutritional product. I took it for two weeks and have never had a back problem since!   Eureka!

## My plan for improvement

I...

- studied a variety of leading edge modalities for physical, spiritual and material mastery and transformation.
- found the answer to my question: "How do I know what people really need?" I spent the next year learning an amazing biofeedback technique. That was 23 years ago. Now it is my biggest gift.
- discovered I have a unique ability to really know what's going on with people on all levels. My knowledge of natural healing plus a way to access innate intelligence is a powerful combination.
- taught people a simple procedure to access their inner knowing using a pendulum. I love helping them rely on their own knowing and know that it is reliable.

## Moving forward my way

I have mastered technologies for going within to access Divine Intelligence. Tapping into that vast wisdom and sharing its gifts and insights is my contribution to those seeking freedom, spiritual connection, love, fulfilment and real answers to the problems and questions of life, health and well-being.

Today, aged 61, I live in Santa Monica, and life is good. Healthy, looking good for a 'young elder', my spiritual life consists of constant contact with the Divine, breathing into ecstasy, and a healthy lifestyle. I am part of a real vision of a Golden Age that begins with us, and we pay it forward.

## Wisdom from along the way

I have learned…

- Even in chaotic and devastating experiences, life is on our side.
- What I bring to the world, and to you perhaps, is a rainbow bridge, a helping hand, a bit of wisdom, and the knowing in your bones that all is well.
- We are powerful beyond our comprehension. As I awaken and progress along the ascending spiral of consciousness, I know my fairy-dust touches and blesses everyone.
- Because we link hearts, hands, and minds, the whole world is healed by love, our love.
- When we trust and maintain our connection with Divine Intelligence, the source from which we arise and to which we are all returning, our experience is a celebration of life well lived. It is as close as the next breath.
- My life is blessed in so many ways. Today, I have gratitude for it all.
- Heaven on earth is possible. It is an inside job, and I would love to walk a while with you.

# Resources to rave about

## Books

*A Course in Miracles*: Combined Volume Dr. Helen Schucman (Foundation for Inner Peace, 2007)

*The Starseed Transmissions* Ken Carey (HarperOne, 1991)

*Return of the Bird Tribes* Ken Carey (HarperOne, 1991)

*The Mayan Oracle: A Galactic Language* of *Light* (revised edition) Ariel Spilsbury (Michael Bryner Bear & Company, 2011)

## Organisations

Agape International Spiritual Center, www.AgapeLive.com, you can watch live services online

# FROM OVERWHELM TO SETTING BOUNDARIES

## CHRISTINA'S STORY
## KNOWING MY BOUNDARIES AND BUILDING SELF-RESPECT

*NAME: CHRISTINA LOUISE*

## About me

Because of my personal experience I consider myself an expert expat with all the necessary survival skills. Originally from Denmark, I lived in Switzerland, France, Spain, China, UK, and Ireland, before coming to Holland where I now live with my Dutch husband and five year-old twins. I'm fluent in English, Danish, French and Dutch. With nine years of corporate experience behind me, I ran a happy but regimented home with two newborns while simultaneously starting my second company and working from my laptop handling web shops, marketing and speaking to customers. I understand the ins and outs as well as pitfalls of building a new business. I am a firm believer in the power of women being master of their lives, both at home and professionally. Today, I coach women entrepreneurs, mothers and expats on how to juggle all their life tasks confidently.

**Website:** www.christinalouise.net
**Email:** christinalouise99@yahoo.com

**Gifts:** A free 45-minute coaching session via telephone or Skype. Sign up for this introductory session on my website www.christinalouise.com

## In the beginning
It was New Year's Eve and I was standing, crystal champagne glass in hand, in front of the TV in my mum's house in France at the foot of Mount Salève, overlooking the beautiful lights of Geneva. We were looking intently at the church tower clock featured on the screen. The sound was low so as to not disturb the friendly chatter in the living room. As my mother is an avid fan of German television, we had tuned into one of their numerous satellite channels broadcasting 'a party in the main square', an image which seemed to strike a chord.

After almost four years of faithful service, I had lost the corporate job I loved as a marketing analyst for an international packaging company though I had suffered that last year, working for a manager who had no respect for me. It had taken all my courage to try networking my way to a *new* job. I decided to open my heart to Ray, my contact with one of my former data suppliers.

"I'll speak to the people in the office," he said, to my surprise.

Consequently, within a few weeks I was invited to an interview in Basingstoke. As I slowly stepped out of the car in front of the intimidating grey metallic building, I tried to convince my pounding heart and shaking hands to calm down. Two distinguished middle-aged gentlemen with white and grey hair received me and their joviality put me at ease. I quickly realised that my main struggle was trying to understand the rolling Scottish accent of Mr Mackay – one of the partners in the company – as he quickly announced: "We'd love to work with you, Christina. You can do our annual and quarterly reports for the UK and Denmark. However, you will work as a freelancer and will have to start up your own company."

Start my own company? This was a scenario that had never occurred to me. It felt frightening and impossible. I had always imagined myself being welcomed into the arms of a corporation that would cherish and value me for life.

It took months but I was now registered as self-employed. Voilà! I had scored the best job in the world: was paid a handsome daily rate giving an annual salary well above any previous earnings and forty weeks holiday per year! How difficult could it be?

One minute to midnight. The clocks on the German church tower started to ring with a baritone 'dong, dong'.

My stomach churned with an ugly feeling of nervousness, loneliness, desperation and anger. The best job in the world had turned sour. The last three months had been filled with endless days of number crunching and staring at Excel spreadsheets while dressed in pyjamas in my tiny 'office', comprised of a wobbly table with a laptop squeezed under the winding stairs in my house. This monotony had been broken only by the highlight of telephone calls to people who were either cold towards me, refused to speak to me or, at worst, screamed insults at me and hung up. My work on the next quarterly report was looming and I just couldn't face it. I felt completely isolated not just by the home-working pattern but because, at the age of 29, I had just moved to live on my own for the first time in my life.

"Happy New Year!" My mother was before me, reaching out to me with a big smile.

"Happy New Year! Let's hope for a healing and wholesome year ahead." We embraced each other.

It was time to make some serious decisions about my future.

## My Turning Point

I realised I had created a pattern of letting people disrespect me and that this had led to me disrespecting myself. I made an important decision that night: *I will no longer work with people who overstep my boundaries, disrespect me or who are just plain and simply unfriendly, unkind or out to beat me down.*

Making a solemn vow to start practising my newfound self-respect, I drafted an email to Mr Mackay that night to say that I was resigning. My heart felt heavy because it had taken months to set up my company and this job was my only source of income.

---

## Taking stock

At my Turning Point I knew my choices were…

- I could accept that a job is just a job and that most people don't enjoy what they do, and be happy with the money despite hating the work.
- Be patient and keep going. Perhaps my loneliness and desperation was only a passing phase until I got used to the job?
- I could tell the people who were screaming at me on the phone that I would not accept their behaviour and hope that they would still give me the information I was looking for.
- I could be honest with myself and acknowledge that I was dealing with a more fundamental issue of self-respect and setting of limits which I needed to work on.

---

## Making it happen

As I pressed the SEND button, I immediately felt as light as a feather and able to breathe freely again. In response and much to my surprise, Mr Mackay invited me to lunch at the luxurious Randolph Hotel in Oxford.

"Tell me about your dream job," he said. I explained my deep need to mentor and inspire others, to impart knowledge, as well as my love for travel and my decision not to work with disrespectful people.

Suddenly, in his beautiful rolling Scottish accent, he asked: "Would you like to take a trip to China for us?" My heart skipped a beat. A dream come true! I subsequently made two research trips to China and one to Singapore.

I also had my own company set up and could look at taking on other exciting projects as they came along. Finally I was reaping the rewards of making the decision to respect myself.

## My plan for improvement

I...

- On the emotional side:
  - made a pact with myself that I do not HAVE to work with people I don't like or who don't like me ever again. They only bring poison into my life.
  - paid attention to and stopped making excuses for other people who overstepped my personal boundaries; this is not okay.
  - valued my personal integrity and respected my own value as a person above outside factors such as money or security.
- On the practical side:
  - found other sources of income. I found translation work online for various companies.
  - contacted the place I had studied marketing and was immediately hired to teach one evening per week which also helped with the income.
  - started a project for myself. I joined the local amateur operatic society to increase my social network and get in touch with my emotions and creativity.

## Moving forward my way

Since those days of working for Mr Mackay's company back in 2000, I feel a different person. For one thing, I changed country to settle with my new husband in Utrecht where the twins were born in 2005. The greatest change is in myself; self-respect and setting boundaries forms part of a more extensive value system I have discovered about myself. Learning about my core values has given me a great sense of purpose and has helped me prioritise my life according to my personal vision. Now I do what I enjoy most, helping women through coaching to discover their values and implement them in their own lives in order to gain fulfilment and gain a clear sense of purpose in their lives.

## Wisdom from along the way

I have learned…

- Determine your own value system. What is acceptable to you? How far are you willing to let other people cross your value system?
- Nothing is worth compromising your own value system for: not money, security or any other outside apparent benefit.
- Be honest with yourself. If you disagree, or dislike a situation, then accept your feelings. Your gut instinct is usually right. Don't make excuses.
- Be scared and do it anyway. Once you have identified the problem and have determined how to fix it, then be brave and speak your mind with courage and confidence.

- Never be solely dependent on one source of income. Find alternative streams of income. This could be true whether you are currently employed or have your own business.

## Resources to rave about

### Books
*The 4-Hour Work Week: Escape the 9-5, Live Anywhere and Join the New Rich* Timothy Ferris
(Vermillion www.rbooks.co.uk, 2011)

*I Can Make You Rich* Paul McKenna
(Transworld Publishers www.rbooks.co.uk, 2008)

*The Soul Millionaire* David J Scarlett
(Summertime Publishing, 2011)

### Web
Alibaba.com, www.alibaba.com, a wholesale website where you can buy just about anything direct from the manufacturer or the wholesaler

Peopleperhour.com, www.peopleperhour.com, a website for freelancers. Find freelance jobs or hire freelancers to help you

Elance.com, www.elance.com, spend your precious time on the things that you are good at and that matter; get yourself a virtual assistant to do the rest

# FROM OUT OF CONTROL TO
# HEALTHY AND HAPPY

## *KELLY'S STORY*
## *RECLAIMING MY BODY, MY FAMILY, AND MY LIFE*

## *NAME: KELLY CORNELL*

## About me

I grew up in San Jose, California and still live in the Bay Area because I love it! As a holistic nutrition coach, I specialize in helping women over forty improve their health, lose weight permanently without dieting, boost their energy, prevent disease, and live life to its fullest. I encourage women all over the globe to heal their bodies through the medicinal power of food. I teach them how to make time for self-care, reduce stress, eat healthy on the go, honor their body and get the lean, sexy figure they truly desire. I am married to an amazing man and we have four beautiful children. My family is all-important and I cherish every moment I have with them. Moving into my late forties, I relish looking and feeling better than ever and am often told that I look ten – and sometimes even twenty – years younger than I am.

**Website:** www.kellycornellwellness.com
**Email:** Kelly@kellycornellwellness.com

**Gifts:** A coupon for $50 off my popular home study program, "Whittle Your Waist in 30 Days or Less". Enter the coupon code: TURNING POINT upon checkout to receive your discount. Visit my website www.kellycornellwellness.com to register for your program and pick up my free report on "The 7 Biggest Mistakes Women Make when Trying to Lose Weight and how to Avoid Them" and sign up for my free inspirational ezine!

## In the beginning

The phone rang. My mother's laughter filled the house as she played with my two-year-old twins in the next room. Listening to the person on the phone, I knew instantly my life would never be the same. Taking a deep breath, I heard my voice, as if for the first time: "Enough is enough – it's time to take charge of my life."

I had been living a lie that somehow had turned into a nightmare.

It all began when I gave up on a lifelong dream – at the age of 18 – to become an actress and performer. Having discovered the Hollywood scene was nothing like I expected, I was terrified of being away from my family and felt a failure because I just couldn't cut it there.

Walking away from all I ever wanted was devastating. Unfortunately, the place I turned to was the refrigerator and, not surprisingly, I packed on the pounds. Almost overnight, the naturally slim dancer ballooned into a chubby girl with a puffy face and a big butt I barely recognized. She had also stopped smiling.

My health took a turn for the worse. Before I knew it, I had a blood sugar imbalance, adult acne, rosacea, irritable bowel syndrome, frequent debilitating headaches, vertigo, a stomach ulcer, and intense PMS. And it wasn't just bloating and mood swings either. The 'irregular' menstrual cycles I had suffered since puberty became a raging hormonal issue called polycystic ovarian syndrome (PCOS) – a number-one cause of female infertility. I was distraught.

My body was falling apart. The junk I ate was literally sucking the life from me. I used food, like a junkie uses drugs, to dull my senses and make me feel good when I felt alone, scared, angry, resentful, and unloved. Food was my reward every time I 'deserved' it.

Eventually I became a sugar addict and always made sure I had easy access to my favorite candies, ice cream and cookies. Like most women, I tried to fix it by going on diet after diet; I essentially tortured myself as I under-ate, over-exercised, and took diet pills.

I felt so disgusted with myself that I hated looking in the mirror. Where was that beautiful dancer? And who was this ugly, out-of-control woman staring back at me?

When my doctor looked me straight in the eye and told me I might never have children due to PCOS, the floor dropped from beneath me. I had married at age 21 to start a family. I was meant to have children.

In my quest to become a mother, I adopted a two-year-old rambunctious towhead with a smile that knocked me over. Then, I tried nearly every infertility treatment available and, against all odds (and without IVF), I got pregnant and had two precious babies – a boy and a girl.

This was a bittersweet time. My marriage was crumbling, a secret I had kept from friends and family, pretending everything was fine. My then-husband was spiraling down into dependence on legal drugs, chronic anxiety attacks and deep depression.

The longer we were together, the worse it got. He'd had a tough life, it wasn't his fault; however, he refused help and was in complete denial. Eventually, his descent into the abyss dragged us all down. He was arrested for embezzlement. We lost our jobs. His car was repossessed. We were evicted from our home and had to file for bankruptcy.

Night after night, I lay awake wondering, 'What's next? What *could* be next?' And although I blamed him for the stress that was destroying my health, I knew I had no one to blame but myself.

## My Turning Point

The school secretary called to say that my then-husband had picked up my son's last bottle of Ritalin. I can still hear the pity in her voice and feel the knot in my stomach as her words sank in.

I knew he was addicted to Ritalin; I had read the books about co-dependency and attended Al-Anon meetings. Yet I was allowing my children's father to take our family down with him.

Something had to change, but I was so mentally, emotionally and physically exhausted I didn't know what to do…

## Taking stock

At my Turning Point I knew my choices were…

- I could keep doing what I was doing, cover up the Ritalin incident and keep making excuses.
- I could give up and simply watch while life spun out of control.
- I could keep blaming my then-husband for ruining all our lives.
- Or, I could regain control of my health and reclaim my life once and for all.

## Making it happen

As soon as I hung up the phone with the school secretary, I came clean with my mom and asked if the kids and I could move back home temporarily. She agreed and within just a few hours we had packed up my mini-van and were out of there.

That day I vowed to take complete responsibility for the rest of my life. I vowed to stop abusing my body and get to the root of my health and weight problems for good. Not just for me, but also for my family.

Three months later, my kids and I moved into a tiny apartment of our own. I enrolled in college to study nutrition full-time and worked part-time. It wasn't easy, but I worked my tail off, knowing that in the long run my kids and I would be stronger and healthier for it.

## My plan for improvement

I…

- read hundreds if not thousands of books and articles on nutrition, health and wellness.
- became my own human science experiment as I tried everything I learned to see what worked and what didn't.
- learned to manage stress and reach out for support.
- discovered what foods were most healing to my body, and ate more of them.
- graduated from college with honors and earned my bachelor's degree in nutritional science.
- reached out to several alternative practitioners who helped me take my health to the next level and taught me the benefits of taking a holistic approach to healing my body and losing weight.
- graduated from the world's largest nutrition school, IIN, and became a certified holistic health coach.
- hired several coaches to support me with my personal growth and development, business and finances.

- healed my body, lost weight and made a commitment to share what I learned with others.
- opened the doors to 'Kelly Cornell Wellness' so I could support women who struggle with their weight, and teach them how to stop dieting and take a holistic approach to health.
- joined a community of like-minded holistic practitioners and coaches to surround myself with positive, loving energy on a daily basis.

## Moving forward my way

My life is completely different. I begin and end each day reflecting on the things I am grateful for. I live in an abundance of peace, joy and love, knowing that I create my life the way I want it to be. Life doesn't happen to me. I am the author of my own life's masterpiece.

My mission is to touch the lives of hundreds of thousands of women, inspiring and motivating them to learn to love the food that loves them back. I assist them in loving and honoring their bodies wherever they are on their journey towards greater health.

## Wisdom from along the way

I have learned…

- Life is a work in progress. Embrace every step along the way.
- Be honest with yourself. There is no shame in confronting your truth.

- Food can be your best friend or your worst enemy. Discover the healing power of food and your life will never be the same.
- Reach out for support. Going it alone is misery.
- Setbacks along the way are learning opportunities. Embrace them.
- Surround yourself with individuals who lift you up and reflect the love in your heart.
- Share your learning with others and you become a beacon of light and hope.
- Everything you need is within. Dig deep inside and you will find peace, harmony, joy, love and light. I promise you this.

## Resources to rave about

### Books
*The World's Healthiest Foods: Essential Guide for the Healthiest Way of Eating* George Mateljan (George Mateljan Foundation, 2007)

*The Big Leap: Conquer Your Hidden Fear and Take Life to the Next Level* Gay Hendricks (HarperOne, 2010)

### People
Louise Hay, www.louisehay.com, learn how to change your thoughts

### Organisations
Institute for Integrative Nutrition, www.integrativenutrition.com, I love the school I graduated from!

# FROM JUGGLING CORPORATE MUM TO JUGGLING BUSINESS OWNER

## *JULIA'S STORY*
### *HARNESSING THE CREATIVITY AND ENERGY IN THE CHAOS OF TRANSITION TO JUST "GO FOR IT"*

## *NAME: JULIA CARTER*

### About me

I hope my story will empower mums who are juggling their role as a mum with their career, or perhaps wanting to return to work after taking time out to have a family. I hope it will ignite a spark within other mothers out there – whether in current work or not – and encourage them to go for it too!

I have two young children and live in Newbury, West Berkshire, UK. Since 2009, I have been growing my own business, Zestfor Ltd, which provides personal development through training and coaching. One of my key areas of focus is career coaching, where I work with people from all over the world who want to escape from their current position or career and discover the right career or job for them. I do this using a selection of tools that are chosen depending on the individual's end goals.

**Website:**  www.zestfor.com
www.zestformondays.com
**Email:**  Julia@zestfor.com

**Gift:** 45-minute coaching session by Skype or phone or an introductory online career coaching module. Please email me to find out more.

## In the beginning

I loved science at school, which led to my studying pharmacy and eventually working as a pharmacist in a well-known pharmacy chain. But this led to my first big career decision – after three years I realised this was not what I wanted to spend the rest of my life doing. I bravely left the career I had spent so many years of my life studying for and joined a global pharmaceutical company. This is where I then spent the next 14 years of my professional life. After three years, I worked my way into my dream job as a learning and development consultant (some may call this a trainer), and this is where I developed as a professional.

The next eleven years saw the birth and evolution of my new career entwined with the birth of my two children. So I now found myself with the new challenge of juggling these two very important parts of my life. Of course, I had that working mother guilt – feeling I was doing a mediocre job at work and a mediocre job at home, but I was fortunate to work for a forward-thinking company that allowed me to work three days a week from the day I returned to work after having my first child. And this is what I did for the next six years. I juggled. My husband worked in London so was effectively out of the equation in the mornings and evenings. Getting two young children up and out by 7.45 on a Monday morning, dropping them at daycare and then driving 25 miles to work at times seemed crazy, but at others felt so normal and empowering. I look back now at the chaos that often reigned on those work-day mornings. Sometimes running so late, I would give my children a piece of toast each to eat in the back of the car on the way to daycare!

I loved getting into work on a Monday morning, being the professional, getting my coffee and sitting down at my own desk – alone – with no interruptions. I loved the adult chat. But there was always that internal guilt – was I being a bad mother? Was I being selfish?

Fortunately my children thrived at daycare, but of course I did occasionally have strong guilt pangs at leaving them there for nearly 10 hours a day. But it seemed to work – for me and for the children – and we all got on with it. But I always knew that this wouldn't and couldn't last for ever. If I was being honest with myself, my career had stagnated now; I was not really developing, but I still loved the role and the people I worked with, so why would I ever choose to change the status quo? I realised how lucky I was to have a good job in a large corporation on a part-time basis.

## My Turning Point

This part-time working lasted for the latter six years of my corporate career, and I felt very, very lucky to be able to work three days a week and be a traditional mum the remaining four days of the week. I guess you could say I had the best of both worlds, although it didn't always feel that way!

In 2009 though, this all came to an end when downsizing and restructuring was occurring around the world. My time was up, my role was disappearing and this was the moment when I had to make some decisions.

### Taking stock

At my Turning Point I knew my choices were...

- I could choose to be the victim and wallow in my own self-pity also aware that my husband was about to be made redundant too.
- I could believe that everything happens for a reason.
- I could become that stay-at-home mum I often wondered about, and do it properly.
- I could become a maths or science teacher – something that I had often considered doing – and knew I would get accepted on the course.

- I could take that leap of faith and fulfil my long-term dream of going it alone – it was now or never.
- I could take control and make some decisions – my decisions.

## Making it happen

My emotions during this period remain vivid. I had trained many delegates in managing change, sharing the emotional reactions experienced during transition. Being so familiar with the theory, I naively thought I wouldn't experience this myself.

Wrong! But because of my knowledge, I recognised the creativity that can come from within, the energy along with the chaos. This was the part I loved and wished I could bottle for the future. During this phase, I came up with my business name, Zestfor. Clients always said I had such a zest for life, a contagious energy, and it just came to me during one mundane drive to the office.

Don't get me wrong – it wasn't an easy decision. I spent many weeks, researching recruitment agencies and training roles, but interestingly never actually applied for anything. I knew deep down that I had to follow my dream. It was now or never.

## My plan for improvement

I...

- reminded myself of my strengths and used them.
- took that risk – if I didn't do it now, I would always wonder…..
- started networking with people that had successful small businesses.
- went to networking meetings and learned.
- embraced the learning curve I would find myself back on.
- felt the fear and did it anyway.
- became an identity – got a logo, website, business cards.
- invested wisely in support and training.
- did not make rash decisions.
- found a peer to share the challenges and the successes with.
- found a coach of my own.
- embraced technology and kept up with the latest developments in my area.

## Moving forward my way

So there I was, suddenly, for the first time in my working career, sitting at home on a working day, alone – another novelty – as my youngest had started school. That first official day as Director of Zestfor Ltd felt strange but so empowering. As my own boss, I could do what I wanted, when I wanted.

That was two years ago. Zestfor is growing, I am growing and I love what I do, which has a positive effect on my husband, children and well-being. For the first time I can honestly say I have a zest for every Monday morning!

## Wisdom from along the way

I have learned...

- Take control of anything it is possible to control – however small – and let go of the stuff that is not within your control.
- Understand the change curve and the associated emotions, and then accept that experiencing these emotions is normal.
- Maximise the good things about working for yourself and minimise the not so good.
- Go with your gut – if it feels right, it probably is.
- When you are feeling disillusioned, you are probably tired. Recognise this, go to bed and wake up fresh – tomorrow is another day.
- Build and use your network.
- Ask for guidance, help and advice – people are so generous; accept this generosity when it is offered but then make your own decision on what feels right.
- Invest in yourself – in your development.
- Surround yourself with positive people.
- Share your successes with anyone who will listen.

# Resources to rave about

**Books**
*Feel the Fear and Do It Anyway* – Susan Jeffers (2011)

**Web**
The internet! Surf, surf and surf – you will be amazed at what you find
LinkedIn / Facebook/ Twitter.

**People**
Other working mothers who are managing to successfully juggle too

# FROM FINANCIAL RUIN TO SUCCESS AND EMPOWERMENT

## ANA'S STORY
## GAINING EMPOWERMENT AND SUCCESS FROM FINANCIAL RUIN

## NAME: ANA POIRIER

## About me

In reading my story, you'll discover that I have a unique ability to overcome adversity. I share my secrets with busy, stressed and tired women who struggle with health issues and find the energy and joy they seek as they build a business, nurture a family, look to attract the perfect partner, or simply feel better. I have been empowering women (and some men) to embody their dreams by prioritizing their physical, mental and spiritual health – their most valuable asset.

Using the very tools I share in my virtual programs, one-on-one coaching, retreats, and writing, I am living my dream life! Originally from Connecticut, I now work from home in Monterey, California, one of the most beautiful places on the planet, supporting women in transforming their health and their lives, taking plenty of time to enjoy hiking, yoga and breathing in the beauty of life from my perch by the sea.

**Website:** www.YogaBodyNutrition.com
**Email:** Ana@YogaBodyNutrition.com

**Gifts:** Free report: '8 Essential Secrets to Jumpstart Your Energy & Transform Your Health', ezine subscription loaded with insider tips, articles, delicious recipes and support for living an energized life in a healthy body you love. www.YogaBodyNutrition.com

## In the beginning

Our loan agent wrung her hands nervously, doing her best to appear calm as we waited for the fax. I closed my eyes, trying to focus on my breath, but noticed the constriction in my stomach, which had become all too common over the last few months. This was our final hope. Anita knew this. And as a friend, she wanted it almost as much as we did.

The elation of our first year of homeownership and watching our investment increase in value by $100,000 was now a distant memory. In fact, what once had seemed like a dream had become nothing short of a nightmare.

Anita looked down at the papers that had just arrived. Her face told the story more clearly than any words ever could.

"Ana. Matthew. I'm so sorry; the bank will not refinance this loan."

My stomach dropped to the floor; this was our last hope, the only way we could stay in the home we had grown to love with its lush, Big Sur-like backyard and generous Meyer lemon tree. I felt a dizzying queasiness as the reality sunk in.

This home had been a safe nest for us to grow, love and enjoy. The leisurely lunches soaking up the California sun on our custom-designed patio, watching the hummingbirds flit around the passionflower, the sunset over the Pacific from the living room window... I saw these memories swirl down the drain of reality.

"Everyone's feeling this real estate crisis; you're not alone." These words did little to comfort the ache in my heart. They simply pulled me back to the overwhelming sense of defeat in the present moment. We would hear them repeated many times in the coming months. As if knowing that others were also watching the places they called 'home' slip through their fingers would make it easier. It didn't. In fact it made it worse.

Being part of the masses – as it turned out – hurt rather than helped our attempts to negotiate with the banks. Indeed, some days I got off the phone exhausted, feeling that my own personal trauma was just one in a sea of many others. I would be left to stew in a pot of frustration and debilitating defeat as no one seemed to offer any solutions or even to care. On one occasion, fury raced through my blood as a bank rep suggested perhaps we had been greedy in purchasing outside our means.

The truth was, we had not been greedy. We, like all those faceless others in the same position, had been naïve and given no reason to doubt our investment. Like most young couples buying their first home, we rode high on the wave of hope. We also truly believed that things would work out before the loans adjusted and the payments nearly tripled.

"We have three years to decide how to move forward, and then we can sell the house or refinance," Matthew had pointed out with complete confidence. No one had any reason to expect the worst.

"Don't you want to stop throwing money out the window on rent?" the loan agent had inquired with an almost cocky air.

Of course, these had both made perfect sense at the time to my slightly naïve grasp of real estate economics. Prior to Mathew planting the seed of homeownership, I never had given this any consideration. I saw it as something I would do later when 'I grew up'. I was inexperienced and young, and felt silly for doubting, even for a moment, that this would work out.

## My Turning Point

The stress of not knowing how to meet the enormous monthly payments seemed unbearable. I had many dark moments meeting my intimate old friends – depression and anxiety.

Yet something shifted one night as I lay awake. I realized I had the power of choice – to say "no" to the bank which refused to work with us, and stop sending them money. I resolved not to dissolve along with the economy. Although part of me felt utterly defeated, another part knew about gifts in adversity and rose to the occasion. I called upon inner strength, awakened years earlier after the sudden death of my father, and the heart-wrenching decision was made.

## Taking stock

At my Turning Point I knew my choices were…

- I could do everything possible to make the payments happen, even though they exceeded our monthly average earnings.
- I could allow my shame around this nightmare to bring me back to the depression I had known all too well just a few years back, make myself sick, and slip into defeated victimhood.
- We could pack up our things and run away to Mexico – simply flee the banks and society.
- Or I could use all the yogic tools I teach, explore all the options for assistance and work this out. I was young, healthy, had a solid business that I loved and understood that I DO have control over my reality.

## Making it happen

Since overcoming my own depression and health challenges, watching my inner and outer world begin to transform as I consciously took charge of my thoughts, my body and my desires, I had learned that we are the creators of our own reality. If I behaved, talked, and thought as if I saw myself as a victim, then I would be a victim. I saw so much more for my life than to be swallowed up by this real estate bubble bursting.

Once connected to that empowered self, I vowed to make it happen, to do whatever was necessary to have the best possible outcome. This included staying committed to the best tools I had: my yoga practice, eating the best healthy foods possible, getting out into nature and making sure I still 'took care of myself'. I needed the strength, resilience and peace of mind these invaluable tools have to offer.

## My plan for improvement

I...

- acknowledged that I have a particular strength for overcoming adversity, then taught my clients to do the same.
- worked on what I could control: my mindset = having gratitude for all that I DO have – a healthy body, sound mind, supportive partner, family and friends...
- began studying marketing and ways to create passive and residual income, which led to my first ebook that I could sell online.

- began a monthly newsletter to generate greater connection, trust and communication with my current, past and potential clients.
- created referral partners, and nurtured mutually beneficial relationships.
- developed cutting-edge group coaching programs, which allowed me to gather more clients, do the same work, and leverage my time for greater income and to help more people.
- became aware that I needed to speak out to help others. I needed to get over my shame and fear of judgement about my situation and money in general.
- resolved to get educated about money and real estate, and reach out to others who could help.
- became clear that the tools I teach others in yoga and holistic nutrition were what I needed most at this time of crisis to stay sane, healthy and be a believable role model for my clients. In taking care of myself in this way, I would save money! These tools included:
- committing to daily yoga, meditation, movement and enjoying nature.
- taking advantage of inexpensive, fresh, organic produce at the farmers' market and preparing simple, delicious food at home (restaurants were out of the budget).
- continuing to communicate, honor and share love within my relationship even when the stress seemed unbearable.
- budgeting everything possible to continue to work with my coaches around health, as I realised this was THE KEY to being able to move forward and be successful... not to mention feel good and attract clients.

## Moving forward my way

This nightmare proved the value of what I teach: when you take exquisite care of yourself, you are empowered and energised to do anything!

Deciding to return the house to the bank, I made a conscious choice to take control of my physical, mental and emotional health, instead of allowing outside circumstances to defeat me. The experience gifted me with the fearlessness to take life's reins, ask for what I want, and trust myself.

My business and my life have never been better. I plan to continue helping women all over the globe take care of their most important investment– themselves.

## Wisdom from along the way

I have learned…

- No 'circumstance' is more important than physical, mental, emotional health. It's just not worth letting it go.
- No financial crisis is more important than love for yourself and your loved ones. Blaming, arguing, finger-pointing only make things worse and will contribute to physical, mental, emotional breakdown.
- Gratitude and positive mindset are the keys to attracting what you want. You CAN have ANYTHING, as long as you believe you can.
- In all adversity there exists a (sometimes very hidden) gift.

- Just because you fail or fall once (or twice or three times...) does not mean success is not right around the next corner.
- It is vital to educate yourself and look at all options and scenarios.
- Never be afraid to ask for what you want.
- If you go down one path and meet a wall, then try another. If you hit a wall again, keep trying. Possibilities are infinite.
- Do not be afraid to invest in yourself. The truth is, you can't afford NOT to invest in the right experts, coaches and guidance.
- Never be afraid to share your story; there is always someone who can learn, benefit or help.

# Resources to rave about

## Books

*Ask and it is Given: Learning to Manifest Your Desires* Esther and Jerry Hicks (Hay House Publishing, 2005)

*A Course in Miracles* (combined Volume) (Foundation for Inner Peace, 1975)

*The Eight Human Talents: The Yogic Way to Restore the Balance of Serenity within You* Gurmukh Kaur Khalsa (Harper Collins, 2000)

*Illuminata: A Return to Prayer* Marianne Williamson (Riverhead Trade, 1995)

# FROM DYSFUNCTIONAL FAMILY TO INTERNET MARKETING MILLIONAIRE

## *RACHEL'S STORY*
## *WHAT NOBODY THOUGHT COULD EVER HAPPEN*

## *NAME: RACHEL ROFÉ*

## About me

My name is Rachel Rofé and I live in Ashland, Oregon – a small hippie town about 11 miles north of California. I'm getting married to my dream man on June 5, and at 28 years old, am co-running a million-dollar internet business from my computer. I've helped thousands of students worldwide online and can literally work from anywhere and still make money. And while things are great right now, it wasn't always that way. Just a few years ago I would have NEVER thought this possible. If you'd like to learn more about internet marketing and how you could use it to develop the life of YOUR dreams, please let me know. I'd be honored to walk with you on your path.

**Website:** www.RachelRofe.com
www.RadiatingRoyalty.com
**Email:** rachelreports@gmail.com

**Gifts:** I will give a copy of 'Happy Outsourcing', my outsourcing guide, to anyone who emails rachelreports@gmail.com and requests a copy ($24.95 value). Free bonus – 'Top 7 Ways You Can Start Feeling Like Royalty NOW!' by signing up at RadiatingRoyalty.com. Please also feel free to drop by my blog at RachelRofe.com and ask me any question you think I can help with. I will do my best to answer it!

## In the beginning

I grew up in an extremely volatile household. My father was severely bipolar and literally supposed to be in a mental asylum. My mother was severely depressed. A psychic once told me my parents should have never had children.

My father had massive mood swings. When things were good, things were great, but when he was in a bad mood, I had no idea what would happen. In the best case, he'd go ballistic and open closets, throw things all over the place, and scream. At other times he'd physically abuse my mom, sister, brother, or me. Whenever something in him 'snapped', he'd just go and go and wouldn't stop.

He'd push one of us to the floor and just kick, scream, and keep going. In even darker times, he raped me. On at least one occasion I have memories of my mom either being there or knowing it was happening… but she knew she couldn't say anything or she'd get hit too.

Even with that said, I still felt like my father's favorite. I was constantly trying to calm him down so that he wouldn't 'snap', and so I lived a great deal of my childhood on eggshells.

By seventh grade, I was 250 pounds and extremely shy. I hated myself so much that I wouldn't shower or brush my teeth for weeks. And while this may sound chaotic, it was all I knew – at least I was used to it. But one day, things got even worse.

My father was at his office with my mother and sister when he snapped – this time worse than usual. He got so mad at my mom that he literally shoved her head through the wall. On the way home, he tried driving into oncoming traffic. My 11-year-old sister had to squeeze through the middle car console and turn the wheel around to save everyone's lives.

After that, my sister called the police. My mom reported my father, thinking he would get help, but he fled to Israel instead. I wasn't home when this happened so never got to even say goodbye. I came back to find every trace of my father completely missing.

The same year, my mom introduced me to her new boyfriend (who went on to become my stepdad). I absolutely hated him from the start and even tried running away a few times. It didn't work though and I ended up having to move in with him.

My stepfather was also physically abusive and hit me any time he decided I did anything wrong. My mom never said anything. One time he was hitting me so much that I went hysterical and called the police. Knowing that they were coming to help me, I took a deep breath and calmed down. By the time the policeman got there, I had calmed myself down so much that he thought I was lying. He said, "Can you walk? Can you talk? Then don't bother me."

It was then that I knew I was on my own.

I spent the next few years writing about how much I hated my life and gaining even more weight. High school was very hard. I was afraid to bring friends home (one time my stepfather got mad and kicked my friends out, forcing them to stand in the rain. Talk about embarrassing). And when I wasn't home, my parents would search my room in case I was hiding letters from my father.

Let's just say that until that point, the odds were VERY stacked against me. Nobody would've labeled me as a high achiever.


## My Turning Point

A book encouraged me to attend T. Harv Eker's 'Millionaire Mind Intensive' workshop. At the close, he offered us the chance to push through our fears by breaking wooden arrows against our throats. It sounds insane, but… I did it and felt SO empowered. He mentioned another workshop – 'Warrior Camp' – where we'd do even more crazy-yet-empowering things. Signing up for this $3,000 course changed me in a HUGE way. I did things I would've never dreamed of, had the opportunity to push myself out of my comfort zone, and broke through many boundaries. I left that camp a completely different person.

## Taking stock

At my Turning Point I knew my choices were…

- I could continue down my negative spiral, eating more food, gaining more weight, and becoming even more depressed…
- I could try to run away again (I had two failed attempts under my belt).
- I could become suicidal (it was certainly on my mind quite often).
- … or I could realize that my life was meant to be MUCH brighter, and start pushing myself out of my comfort zone.

## Making it happen

I knew it was time for a change. Up until then I'd always wanted to travel but kept making excuses. Now, following 'Warrior Camp', I was a different person and decided to pack up my car and start a career in internet marketing. Before this I'd been working as a retail manager, in charge of millions of dollars of business for Target. I was like a hamster on a wheel, working 80 hours a week and going to school full-time. I was responsible for up to 300 people at a time and worked so hard that when I quit they hired two people to replace me.

Now, because I had very little money, I was sleeping in my car at Wal-Mart parking lots throughout the country. It was scary, but I felt more alive than I had ever felt before.

---

## My plan for improvement

I...

- pulled over on a highway and signed onto the internet with my air card when I needed to get something done.
- joined Toastmaster's in LA. The first time I spoke I was so nervous that I cried, but after some practice I won 'Best Speaker' on several occasions.
- started losing weight and ended up losing over 100 pounds.
- sold one of my websites. With my earnings I decided to move to Rio de Janeiro for three months and spent the entire time meditating on a beach and really developing my spiritual gifts.
- visited 49 of the 50 states, went back to South America and lived in Buenos Aires for a while.
- developed my business skills whilst travelling, read hundreds of books, got hundreds of thousands of dollars' worth of education, and started working as a professional copywriter.
- did a lot of volunteer work, became a Reiki master, mentored many students, and published a book on meditation.

- started another internet marketing company, and ended up selling that one as well.
- found an amazing new business partner and business took off in a major way. I have been able to do so many things with the money we earn together!

## Moving forward my way

Life is really great. I have a personal chef, two assistants, and a thriving business. I've won an affiliate marketing contest to go to Bali, spoken at conferences throughout the country, and sold two companies – all by the age of 28. My Cornell education couldn't do this for me; it was thanks to learning through experience and being positive that internet marketing helped fuel me.

I've always found I'm WAY happier when experiencing the richness of life and doing business to help people. Now my mentors are not only giving me testimonials but asking ME for business advice. It's incredible!

## Wisdom from along the way

I have learned…

- If you're open-minded enough you'll almost always instinctively get answers.
- Be nurturing with the business, and your happiness levels will definitely increase.
- Ignorance is often the cause of annoyance. Getting a better view on something will improve whatever you're struggling with in life.

- Adopt the 'ripple effect' - do something nice for someone, they'll do something nice for someone else, making the world a happier place.
- What other people think about you doesn't need to concern you. Learn from it or ignore it - don't personalize it.
- It is not 'spiritual' to put others before you all the time. In fact it's pretty fake and doesn't honor your highest self.
- Sitting in pain is FINE ; don't hide from it. I am allowed to feel sad, angry, or hurt and it's a beautiful thing.
- It's perfectly okay to look like a fool.

## Resources to rave about

### Books
*Secrets of the Millionaire Mind, Mastering the Inner Game of Wealth* T. Harv Eker (HarperBusiness, 2005)

*Influence: The Psychology of Persuasion* (Collins Business Essentials) Robert B. Cialdini (Harper Paperbacks, 2006)

*Predictably Irrational: The Hidden Forces That Shape Our Decisions* Dan Ariely (Harper Perennial, 2010)
*The 4-Hour Workweek* Tim Ferriss
(Crown Archetype, 2009)

*Like the Flowing River* Paulo Coelho
(Harper Perennial, 2010)

*The Big Leap: Conquer Your Hidden Fear and Take Life to the Next Level* Gay Hendricks (HarperOne, 2010)

# FROM DISABILITY TO A THRIVING HOME-BASED BUSINESS

## *KATE'S STORY*
## *NEVER GIVE UP NO MATTER WHAT COMES YOUR WAY*

## *NAME: KATE COBB*

## About me

When you've read my story, you'll see that I'm persistent and determined! I use these qualities working with women professionals who are at transition points in their lives, their careers or their businesses and need some support to get them moving forward so they can achieve their desires. I have 30 years' experience empowering women through coaching and training, having been a woman entrepreneur myself since 1986. I help clients get clear on their goals and put powerful action plans into place so they can live the lives they've always dreamed of. Originally from Manchester in UK, I lived in London for many years whilst working internationally and finally came to the South of France 15 years ago. I live with my four cats, who all found me. I am a passionate choral singer and use my management talents as a volunteer to organise choral and orchestral events in the region.

**Website**: www.movingforwardyourway.com
**Email:** kate@movingforwardyourway.com

**Gifts:** Free ebook *Who are YOU?* with exercises to raise your self esteem, and a monthly newsletter which gives you the opportunity to book a complimentary coaching session with me, all available from my website www.movingforwardyourway.com

## In the beginning

I finally found a place to park and glanced at the sunrise over the Baie des Anges. The perfect curve of the bay was always an arresting sight but especially so this morning. The dawn light wrapped the whole of the town of Nice in a warm, pink blanket, which lay way down below me and the hilltop hospital where I had been spending a frightening amount of time. I turned to walk through the sliding doors and find my way to Dr Fabrizi's office. With 18 months of tests behind me, they had finally diagnosed a rare muscle condition with an unpronounceable name that would gradually affect my mobility and, in just a couple of years, possibly leave me in a wheelchair.

"Ah Madame Cobb, *vous avez la chance*! I have managed to get you into the treatment programme," she said; her shiny dark hair swung slightly as she glanced quickly back at her notes.

My palms were clammy. I rubbed them on my trousers.

"It was not easy to do," she said with a smile that showed she was proud her name had opened doors. "In three weeks you will come in every day at 8 o'clock and spend all day on the drip." She looked up and caught my eye. "It doesn't work for everyone, Madame Cobb," she continued.

"I can't do that," I blurted as panic rose in my chest. "I'll be in Jordan in three weeks! I'm training managers there; they are expecting me; it's all arranged." My two worlds collided with a thudding thump.

I was at the height of my career as a training consultant and group facilitator, working on EU and US funded programmes in Eastern Europe and the Middle East. I was hopping on planes twice a month, working with governments and their ministers to prepare them for massive organisational upheavals. This was work that I loved. I had been doing it for over 20 years and couldn't see myself giving it up for a hospital bed and a treatment with no guarantee of a cure.

My thoughts raced ahead. What would happen to my work? How would I cope? Could I even continue? As a single woman I had no one who would support me. I had been freelance for 20 years; if I were to lose my earning power then I would be in serious financial difficulty. I refused to accept what she was saying.

"*Mais* Madame Cobb, *désormais vous devez mener une vie tranquille!*" she advised, picking up a pen and tapping it on her desk. Lead a quiet life? What was she talking about? And as the penny slowly began to drop and clattered on the tiled floor of her consultation room, I realised that my life would never be the same again.

I refused that first invitation to a week in a hospital bed but as time went on, even I could see the deterioration in my body and I went on to spend one week a month for 18 months attached to that drip. Then Dr Fabrizi and her team decided that I wasn't getting enough benefit and removed me from the programme. At 4.30 one October day, I walked very slowly out of the hospital with the black metal stick I now habitually used, a pocket full of prescriptions to get filled at the *pharmacie* and a new *rendezvous* booked for three months' time. I was on my own.

## My Turning Point

Returning home to my hilltop village, I struggled up the steps to get to my three-storey dream house. As I collapsed on the sofa, staring up at the stairs that were becoming almost impossible to climb, I finally faced the fact that I would have to sell my home and find something adapted to my worsening condition. As someone belligerently independent and resolutely single and happy to be so, I had never felt so helpless and alone in my life.

This was my true moment of choice.

**Taking stock**

At my Turning Point I knew my choices were...

- I could just accept the medical diagnosis that 'nothing could be done'.
- Although I was already feeling pretty low, I could continue further into depression and despondency.
- I could completely retire from the world, not go out and live the life of a recluse accepting what little money I could claim in benefits.
- Or I could start an upward spiral of thinking and action to reverse matters.

## Making it happen

I have always believed that however difficult things get, we always have a choice, even if it's only the choice to stay where we are! That was not a choice for me; there was no question of my abandoning everything I had worked for and accepting what I had been told was inevitable.

Having moved to a suitable apartment, I focused on the future prospects and what I really loved doing. The more I worked on this, the more I felt enthusiastic and even energised about the new opportunities I was seeing. I kept the health side in mind as well and decided to explore complementary therapies. Thankfully my brain and my creativity have never been affected so I had that on my side.

Having analysed what I wanted and looked at options, I was ready to establish a plan of action!

# My plan for improvement

I…

- analysed that my strength was, and still is, empowering others.
- decided to develop a coaching business from home that was conducted by telephone.
- booked myself on a coaching course to get a qualification that would back up my 25 years of coaching experience.
- began to see myself as a valuable human being again and not someone labelled 'handicapped'.
- discovered that working from home could be a positive bonus both to me and my clients and that working by telephone is a really powerful coaching tool as well as giving me the chance to work with women all over the world.
- invested in training programmes and coaching packages to learn the skills that I needed to develop for my business
- made opportunities to get myself back to health, including going to California for study.
- transformed my business by placing emphasis on its coaching aspect and not the training role that had been so familiar.
- built a client list and designed innovative online coaching and training programmes, which women can do when they have the time at home using webinar and teleconference technology as well as online training platforms.

- invested regularly in working with four coaches (health, fitness, business, personal); they give me support and keep me motivated by regular sessions and holding me accountable for my actions.

## Moving forward my way

The nightmare is in the past now and I'm looking forward to the future and the increasing success of my business.

I am happy to know I am having a positive influence on other people's lives and their businesses. I've perhaps learnt the hard way, but at least I've learnt and I continue to learn. My health isn't perfect yet, but it's much better and I am thinking of running training courses again which is my next goal. A few years ago I wouldn't have thought this possible but see how far I have come!

## Wisdom from along the way

I have learned...

- No obstacle is so great that you can't overcome it with a change of mind set.
- Even with changed circumstances the essence of what you offer to prospective clients doesn't need to change.
- Learn to ask for, and accept, help – you can't do it all alone and you don't have to.
- Investing in yourself and your personal and business development is invaluable.
- Keeping your body healthy and energetic puts you in the best position to help others.

- It is important to stay ahead of the game and keep up with new technologies.
- Facing up to and conquering your fears will reap untold rewards.
- There are always options and choices.
- You can be better, richer and more creative than you ever thought possible.

## Resources to rave about

### Books
*Money, and the Law of Attraction: Learning to Attract Wealth, Health, and Happiness* Esther Hicks and Jerry Hicks (Hay House, 2008)

*The Big Leap: Conquer Your Hidden Fear and Take Life to the Next Level* Gay Hendricks (HarperOne, 2010)

*Creative Visualization: Use the Power of Your Imagination to Create What You Want in Your Life* Shakti Gawain (New World Library, 2002)

### People
Wendy Harrington, www.wendy-harrington.com, an amazing, inspiring energy healer who has helped me hugely.

# FROM CRIPPLING LOSS TO HEALING AND SUCCESS

## ANN'S STORY
## EMERGING FROM AN ECLIPSE

### NAME: ANN MITCHELL

## About me

After reading my story I hope you will applaud my tenacity, especially in holding on to the belief that 'I will be okay'.

We all have many roles in life and are many things to many people; my proudest roles are as mum and grandmother. My children and grandchildren are my joy and I consider myself blessed.

Born in St Andrews (the home of golf), Scotland, enjoying an outdoor, stress-free childhood on a farm, I was an only child. Were they here today, I hope my wonderful, intelligent mother and very strict disciplinarian father, both of whom shaped the woman I have become, would be proud of my achievements after enormous upheaval and heartbreak.

I help small to medium-sized organisations run their businesses more effectively, lifting the weight from their shoulders and doing business management, bookkeeping, administration, PA and secretarial services: all the backroom 'stuff' that blocks the flow of revenue.

**Website:**  www.annmitchellmanagement.co.uk
**Email:**    ann@annmitchellmanagement.co.uk


## In the beginning

We were a family with businesses. My father, my mother, my husband and I were all working together in the dairy business in Edinburgh, Scotland. We were fairly successful, very happy and enjoyed a good standard of living. My children never wanted for anything and we had lovely family holidays, sometimes to exotic places. My father had a farm and my family would spend Sundays there, once again in an outdoors environment.

Then, on a lovely summer day in July 1992, it all dramatically changed when my mum collapsed and died at the age of 61 years. We lost our anchor. My father was devastated. I had never seen him cry before and this was heart-wrenching in itself. From that day onward, he did not go back to work in the dairy and decided to shift direction and change the farm into a golf course...

This was the beginning of the end. The upshot of it all was a demise of the businesses – which was bad enough. However, the personal toll was even greater. The relationship between Dad and me deteriorated because of business conflict. I visited him at the farmhouse, where once we had all sat down to have meals together and where my children used to run round the table playing 'tag', and said, "You know, Dad, when this is all over, I hope we can sit down and talk about it all." His answer was, "I hope so too, Ann, I hope so too."

In 1998, my marriage broke down after 24 years, and my children, Steven and Wendy, then aged 21 and 18, stopped speaking to me. I moved out of the family home and bought a flat. Enough?

My father died suddenly in 1999, without our having had the chance to 'sit down and talk'. The consequences all culminated in businesses being sold. For my part, the business I was most involved with was put into liquidation in June 2000. I was redundant, unemployed, very frightened, 46 years old with not a clue where to turn. I was alone. Enough?

No. The bank had obtained a personal guarantee from me when we were expanding the business and now they wanted their money. They were in effect going to take my home, but that is another story.

Just for now I had no income. No income! I needed a job. Thankfully my mortgage was covered by insurance, so I still had a roof over my head. So, I had to start to be practical: cancel the satellite TV, cancel pension contributions, cut up store cards, sell the car, pay off finance.

I needed a job. The first stop was the local employment office. Now, here was a revelation: fill in forms, answer questions and become a 'case'. Forget that you were once a Financial Director and had a good salary. You are now a 'case' and entitled to job seekers' allowance; come back every two weeks and sign here to claim your benefit. Next!

"Why me?" I wondered. Well, I guess the question is, "Why not me?"

## My Turning Point

Curled up on my bed, the enormity of the whole mess was so crippling I thought I would never stand upright again. I wanted to ignore the ringing telephone, but hoped it might be Steven or Wendy, so dragged myself to answer. It was my cousin Mary. I literally could not speak. She drove over, took me for a walk, bought us a bag of chips and pulled me up a little from my black hole.

Starting to think positively, I refused to be beaten and was surprised to discover I had this steely reserve and the belief that 'I WILL be okay'.

## Taking stock

At my Turning Point I knew my choices were…

- I need to survive and I have to do something.
- Should I just give up and walk away?
- I have a brain and it functions.
- List what I *can* do and what I *do* have and don't dwell on the events of the past.
- *I* alone have to do this; no one else can do this for me.

## Making it happen

A recruitment agent asked, "Why don't you start your own business? You have the skills." I listed my 'skills' and was frankly amazed. I had studied with the OU Business School, but my self-esteem and confidence had disappeared.

I saw an advertisement for a 'Be Your Own Consultant' seminar run by the Business Gateway with Edinburgh Chamber of Commence as an opportunity. If I used my credit card I could pay the £80 fee back monthly. I booked my place and on the day, put on my business suit for the first time in three months! The high heels took time to get used to as I teetered about like a new born lamb, but it still felt good.

The tutor at the seminar also suggested starting my own business with my background and experience. Ann Mitchell Management? The seeds were sown. Business Management and Office Administration. Sounded good!

## My plan for improvement

That day of the seminar, and while the self-belief was high, I…

- started to write my business plan; then
- got clear about what I could do for other people's businesses.
- researched how and where I was going to market myself.
- explored networking strategy through the Edinburgh Chamber of Commerce.
- developed and practised what I would say when introducing the services
- wrote it all down (if it was visible, it had life).
- bought self-development books and read them and learned; then
- carried out the exercises in these books and started to grieve for the losses and finally believed I could do this.
- started a daily journal of ten things to be grateful for.
- never gave up hope.

## Moving forward my way

I submitted my business plan to the Business Gateway and was successful in getting a grant to buy a computer and printer. That was 11 years ago and my business is still going strong. I continue to learn, never taking anything for granted.

The most wonderful achievement is that after five years of not communicating, my daughter Wendy contacted me. A clever, articulate young woman and wonderful mother, since 2009 she has been working with me and is a director of my company.

After seven years, my son and I met up. It was as if we had never lost touch. Never give up!

## Wisdom from along the way

I have learned…

- Don't try to solve everything at once.
- Break it all down into manageable 'chunks'.
- Take ownership – it is about you and yourself – no one else.
- Seek help – don't be afraid to speak about your circumstances or your lack of knowledge.
- By all means listen to advice, but always follow your instincts, nobody else walks in your shoes, so you know what is best for YOU.
- Decide what needs to be tackled first and devise a workable plan to start the change.
- Now you have begun the 'I can' process,
- Begin the 'I will' – I will change things, I will succeed.

# Resources to rave about

**Books**
*Self Matters* Dr Phil McGraw (Simon & Shuster, New York, 2001)

*The Road Less Travelled* M. Scott Peck (Arrow, 1978)

**People**
My family and friends, who never let me fall!

**Organisations**
The local Business Gateway offices – Edinburgh

Edinburgh Business Women's Club, www.esbc.org.uk

Association of Scottish Businesswomen, www.asb-scotland.org

Waterstones Book Shop! When you are going through trying times, take from the books and resources what you need at that time. Hopefully start to learn, grow, plan and in some cases heal.

# FROM FRUSTRATION ABROAD TO A THRIVING PORTABLE CAREER

## LOUISE'S STORY
## COFFEE MORNINGS AND TELECONFERENCES

## NAME: LOUISE WILES

## About me

I'm thrilled to share my story with you, not because it has all turned out perfectly – I am a work in progress! – but as a mother with two young daughters, wife, expatriate and business owner, I know how challenging it can be to balance and succeed in all areas of life, especially when living a mobile and uncertain life abroad. I'm British but have lived 12 of the past 15 years in Spain and Portugal, relocating five times. I understand both the positive and negative impact that successive relocations can have on life. Through my business I offer support to expatriates who are feeling lost and directionless abroad. I help my clients to rediscover themselves, their passions and interests, and build successful mobile careers and businesses abroad. I use my personal experience and professional background in coaching and personal development to devise online programmes, coaching programmes and events.

**Website:** www.successabroadcoaching.com
**Email:** louise@Successabroadcoaching.com

**Gifts:** Access to two teleseminars, PDF scripts of the teleseminars, and workbooks. Access these free gifts by going to this webpage on my website: http://successabroadcoaching.com/clients/
When asked for a password, type in: *turning points*. Once logged in, follow the instructions.

## In the beginning

As the plane touched down, my almost-three-year-old jumped excitedly in her seat, pointing at the sea and exclaiming, "We're here Mummy, we're here in Dadeira." I looked out at the shimmering sea and the isolation of the deserted islands in the distance and shivered.

My husband was reading the newspaper and as we taxied up to the gate he folded it, looked out of the window dispassionately and tidied away the in-flight detritus. How could he be so calm, I wondered as I held back a rising sense of panic, coupled with the all too familiar overwhelming nausea that accompanied me wherever I went: I was four months pregnant.

We stepped down from the plane and onto the soil of our new home. As I walked I fought an internal battle: heart fluttering excitement and exhilaration for the start of a new life, combined with a struggle to hold back the tears as I thought about what we had just left behind. Unaware of her mother's internal battle, my daughter chattered away, pointing at the other planes, excited to be boarding a bus for what turned out to be a disappointingly short journey. I let my shoulders drop, breathed deeply and started looking for the positives. I found a warm, humid sea air and a neat, almost pretty airport, well organised and surprisingly clean. It all felt comfortable and friendly, even familiar. Not a bad start, I decided.

But wait – I am getting ahead of myself. My expatriate story did not begin here in Madeira. It started a full ten years earlier in Spain. Newly married, after a year of a 'commuting' relationship, I finally left my job and did what our family saw as the 'sensible' thing: joined my husband in Madrid.

Attracted by the sun, my husband (of course), the vibrancy of this wonderful Spanish city and the excitement of new beginnings, I remember feeling in those first months a sense of freedom, a lightness and optimism. I had just turned thirty, had had a successful career in the UK and was happily married. I felt I could be and do anything. First things first, learn the language and then enjoy my well earned career break. Sixth months ought to do it, I thought optimistically.

Of course I'd find a job – easily, learn the language – easily, and make lots of Spanish friends – easily. I didn't – and gradually my enthusiasm and excitement gave way to loneliness and frustration. I found my way eventually, but it took time and a number of wrong turns and disappointing starts.

Now, as we arrived in Madeira, I reflected on the thought that we had already recreated our lives three times in the last ten years and here I was starting all over again – again! What's more, this time I was pregnant with my second child and had left all my support systems behind in the UK.

Fast forward one year: new baby, comfortable home, new friends. I was beginning to feel I was getting there – some days. However, there was a nagging sense that I was living someone else's life. A life as a non-working expatriate wife and mother had never been part of my 'grand plan'. While back in the UK I had completed a Master's in Occupational Psychology and just embarked upon a Certificate in Performance Coaching. Moving and giving birth to baby number two had put the course and my career plans on hold. But suddenly, in my fortieth year, I had a sense of passing time, a feeling that it was now or never.

## Turning Point

Was it really sensible to think I could create a new career while living on a tiny rock in the Atlantic, with two children under five? Why not? I had a vision, enthusiasm and belief in what I was doing and wanted to share that with others. Sitting home procrastinating meant I was achieving nothing but personal frustration.

One day, my business coach asked: "When you look back on your life what will be your greatest regret?"

I answered immediately: "My greatest regret will be to have never tried, to have been too scared to give it a go."

---

**Taking stock**

At my Turning Point I knew my choices were…

- I could decide that because we would be moving on again at some unknown future point there would be no point in developing a business or career.
- I could simply decide that this was all my life could and should be and quite justifiably focus all my efforts on my children and family.
- I could look for more local opportunities to fill my time: charitable work, local hobbies, interests and coffee mornings.
- I could choose to think inspiring thoughts about developing my career and my business.

---

## Making it happen

I knew then I had to take the next steps, complete my coaching qualification and turn my vision into reality. I set to and worked at every opportunity; whenever Issy slept I picked up my computer. I squeezed every possible minute out of every day. I completed the course and obtained a distinction; a great confidence booster!

But that was the start and not the end. I decided that I wanted to set up my own online coaching business. I wanted to use my experience and knowledge to help people like me, people for whom relocation is a fact of life and who want to use their experiences in a positive way to build mobile careers and businesses.

First though, I had to create my own business. This is how it happened – and is continuing to happen today – despite another relocation, this time a short hop to Lisbon.

## My plan for improvement

I...

- identified a subject about which I felt passionate.
- researched my market thoroughly by running surveys, reading books, blogs and websites.
- created a vision for my business and personal life that inspires me and gives me my 'reason why'.
- set goals and targets that quite frankly terrify me, BUT excite, inspire, stretch me to work at 'my best'.
- made financial investments that mean I have no option but to succeed.
- set out to understand my strengths and talents. I found this so valuable that I am now a qualified strengths practitioner.
- created an online range of products and services, to reach as many people in the world as possible
- invested in a website, created a blog, issued a twice-monthly newsletter, learnt about social media
- started to outsource some of the more repetitive and administrative tasks.
- recognised that my family is still my priority and learnt to close the door on my business and computer when the kids are around. The two just do not mix!

- found an inspirational business coach who supports, inspires and challenges me.
- recognised that so much of running and promoting a business is about 'mind-set'.

## Moving forward my way

The decision is made and my direction is clear.

I love the work I do; I feel so fortunate to be able to sit down each morning with enthusiasm and real interest in what I do and for the people I work with. I have a big vision about the kind of online community I would like to create: somewhere expatriate partners from all over the world can go to identify and develop their personal passions, careers and businesses; somewhere that supports and inspires everyone to achieve their best – their personal success abroad.

## Wisdom from along the way

I have learned…

- Learn about and understand your strengths and talents then use them to inspire, energise and motivate you.
- Use your opportunity as an expatriate to identify the career or business passion that will enable you to be YOU – your authentic self.
- Be honest with yourself about what you want and what you don't want to be.
- Indecision is the worst place to be. Learn to make decisions and then take fast action.
- Invest in your personal development, health and general well-being.

- Understand what it is that helps you flourish in life.
- Be grateful – stop regularly and note what you feel thankful for in your life.
- Find a mentor or role model, someone who inspires you but also someone you can aspire to be. Model yourself on them.
- If you are a parent abroad, be prepared for the family interruptions that will inevitably come your way: the holidays, the sick child. Build in contingency plans that mean you can be a parent without feeling conflicted all the time.
- Keep focused on your vision, your passions and your reasons why. This is what will get you over the obstacles that will inevitably come your way.

## Resources to rave about

### Books

*Positivity, Groundbreaking Research to Release Your Inner Optimist and Thrive* Barbara Fredrickson
(Oneworld Publications, 2010)

*Feel the Fear and Do It Anyway* Susan Jeffers
(Vermilion, 2007)

*Culture Shock! Successful Living Abroad: A Wife's Guide* Robin Pascoe (Graphics Arts Center 2002)

*A Career in Your Suitcase* Jo Parfitt (Bookshaker, 2008)

*The Millionaire Messenger* Brendon Burchard
(Morgan James, 2011)

*The Big Leap, Conquer Your Hidden Fear and Take Life to the Next Level*, Gay Hendricks (HarperOne, 2011)

# FROM NATURAL NETWORKER TO SOCIAL MEDIA SPECIALIST

## JO'S STORY
## FINALLY FINDING MY IDEAL CLIENTS

### NAME: JO DODDS

## About me

After many years in the Retail HR 'corporate world', I started my own small business in August 2005, publishing a local community magazine in my home town. I expanded the business over the following three years to include, at one stage, eight local British magazines. I still publish the Hythe Handbook with a distribution of 9,000 on a bi-monthly basis, but my main focus now is on helping solopreneurs and small business owners get their business online using a social media model, which generates more leads, prospects and customers through search engine optimisation, blogging, Twitter, Facebook, LinkedIn and YouTube. I live with my husband and five-year-old daughter, and next door to my in-laws, in Hythe, Kent. I love reading and I play netball and the bassoon, but not at the same time!

**Website:** www.jododdssocialmedia.com
**Email:** jo@ jododds.com

**Gift:** FREE online marketing strategy session available from my site
www.jododdssocialmedia.com/work

## In the beginning

I was always an early adopter of the internet – I met my husband on an online dating site in 2002. When I decided to change my business in 2008 the internet was the obvious choice, but the challenge was which aspect of the internet would prove to be my thing?

I spent most of 2008 and 2009 learning internet marketing by attending various conferences and seminars. I also invested a lot of money, that I didn't have at the time, in a mentor to help me become a speaker and business coach. Part of that programme involved me flying to Australia for a two-day training event – how mad was that?! It was such a big commitment, and it marked a Turning Point in my business life – though not exactly turning on a sixpence, more like a large tanker starting to turn.

At the beginning of 2010, I realised that I needed to specialise my business and find a niche in which to succeed. My original plan was to focus on local online marketing as I had experience of running a local business myself, but I couldn't really make that work and I didn't know why. I had a great reputation amongst local businesses in my area, but it was difficult to get them to invest in me. I met a business friend around that time who heard me saying that I didn't think that small local businesses were willing to pay for local online marketing support, and she asked me whether that was a 'limiting belief'. I replied that it had been 'my reality' for the previous year whether or not it was a limiting belief! That same person went on to offer local online marketing coaching and struggled just as much as I had to 'sell her wares'!

So in early 2010 I rebranded myself as a social media specialist. I have always been a strong networker. I went to a school reunion recently; there were around fifty people from my school year, none of whom had been my close friends at school. It was interesting to find out that I knew almost all of them, enough to have a personal conversation and find out what they had been doing since school. So even at school I had been a networker. In 2007 I won 'Networker of the Year' from my local Chamber of Commerce. Online social networking was a natural extension for me.

One of the other challenges I faced, which I think is common for many other female business owners, was my confidence. I used to talk about other people seemingly having 'front' and that if I had that I would be flying! I couldn't really define what 'front' was other than confidence, and I could identify those people who had it even if I couldn't explain what that meant.

In May 2010 something happened that really kick-started an increase in my confidence. I went to a three-day event and met someone whose mailing list I was on. I introduced myself to her and said I was on her list. She was really impressed and said, "Oh wow, the famous Jo Dodds is on my mailing list". I laughed and tried to explain that she must be confused and that I was impressed to be on her list! That person went on to turn over $100,000 in one month a few months later. That whole experience gave me so much more confidence in my business profile and helped me to get some of that 'front' that I was looking for.


## My Turning Point

Each Christmas, we go skiing. The year end is a good time for taking stock of life and planning to make changes into the New Year. So, there I was in December 2010, whooshing down ski runs in gorgeous weather, mulling over my business, what was working and what wasn't.

Recently I hadn't been enjoying my work. What I hadn't realised until skiing down the mountain was how that manifested: waking every morning, dreading the day ahead, feeling like I was in 'a job' working for someone else rather than running my own business. So, what to do?

## Taking stock

At my Turning Point I knew my choices were…

- Carry on offering the same sort of services, such as taking whatever people were asking for, offering it and continuing to earn way below where I needed to be.
- Accept that my business model would always mean providing a 'service' to my clients, which would feel like a 'job'.
- Change my business model to get higher paying clients less interested in a 'service' and more interested in 'mentoring' and 'working with me'.
- Get an actual 'job' (although that wasn't really an option in my mind!).

## Making it happen

Knowing I couldn't carry on working in those circumstances, I had to come up with a different business model.

I decided to review my current clients and assign each of them to a category: 'clients who I loved and would like to work with again' and 'clients who were just draining my energy'. Coupled with that, I decided to work out which areas of my business really got me motivated and which bits didn't.

My mentors had been telling me to put my prices up, and I was still struggling with that concept. The fact that I needed the business meant that I was compromising my business as a result; in other words, I was accepting work that I didn't want because people were offering to pay me for it!

## My plan for improvement

I...

- raised my prices.
- streamlined my business, offering more focused products and services.
- worked only with clients who I felt were a good fit for my business.
- turned work away if it wasn't a good fit with me.
- created a VIP programme for real action takers prepared to invest in their business.
- created a membership site to enable people to 'work' with me at a lower investment but with a much lower expectation of personal service.
- started to outsource the areas of my business that I don't want to do or where I could find people better and cheaper.
- invested in my own learning with mentors who have 'been there and done that'.

## Moving forward my way

This year has snowballed (pun intended!). In two hours in January I sold past my January sales target. In February I started working with clients whose investment in mentoring with me was a stretch for them and they are massive action takers. In March I got my first VIP client.

I now have a team who work with me to deliver a great service to my VIP clients, which leaves me free to work with them in much more of a mentoring role.

My hourly rate more than quadrupled virtually overnight – and better still, I feel very comfortable with that.

---

### Wisdom from along the way

I have learned…

- Higher value clients are action takers and much less demanding than low value clients.
- Know your own value – what is the transformation that you bring about for your clients and what does it mean to them – and charge accordingly.
- Take notice of points along your journey, learn from them and use them as benchmarks.
- Tell stories about your own development – it really anchors your learning and helps you to push further forward.
- Don't give up: the breakthrough is always only just around the corner.
- Become more 'selfish' about your business: decide what you want to do, how and with whom, and make it happen.
- Get your priorities right in your business, and work on what's important – often not what's urgent; get that balance right.

# Resources to rave about

**Books**
*The New Rules of Marketing & PR; How to Use Social Media, Blogs, News Releases, Online Video, and Viral Marketing to Reach Buyers Directly* David Meerman Scott (Wiley, 2010)

**People**
Lisa Sasevich, www.theinvisibleclose.com, 'The Queen of Sales Conversion'

Carrie Wilkerson, www.barefoot-executive.com, The Barefoot Executive

# FROM EMPTINESS TO SPIRITUAL FULFILMENT

## *TARA'S STORY*
## *FINDING A NEW WAY TO CREATE MY LIFE*

## *NAME: TARALYNN MAJESKA*

## About me

When you've read my story, you will see that I am a compassionate optimist who will always find a way to transform the seemingly negative into something positive! I use these qualities to gently guide my students and clients to discover new perspectives in difficult situations – empowering them to create the life of their dreams. I am attuned as a Reiki Master, a Channeler of Divine Messages, a Spiritual Response Practitioner with an Advanced Certificate, as well as a Certified Lifeline Practitioner.

I live in Wisconsin with my husband and two children. My passion is writing and supporting others through the challenges in their lives, into new, remarkable possibilities created with intention. My new book, *When Your Heart is Cracked Wide Open: Navigating with Your Heart through the Challenges of Life,* provides you with the tools to transcend your old patterns into new habits of positive action and attraction.

**Website:** www.majesticilluminations.com
**Email:** tmajeska@charter.net

**Gift:** Call (920)-948-8534 or email tmajeska@ charter.net to make an appointment for a FREE 20-minute Divine Guidance Reading by phone.

## In the beginning

It was the last day of school and I was asking my aspiring eighth grade students, "What would you do if you knew you could not fail?" They were heading off to high school next year, ready to begin a new phase in their lives. I wanted to inspire them to think about their possibilities and focus on a goal to make their dreams come true.

"If you knew that nothing, NO THING, could stand in your way – not money, your educational level, expectations, time or anything else – what would you allow yourself to do?"

It was a question I had considered for myself, and in many ways I had aspired to and accomplished my dreams. I had gone back to school and earned a Bachelor's degree in Education while raising a family and working part-time. Then, I began teaching eighth grade English at a middle school, and within three years I had received my Master's Degree in Education and had been awarded Middle School Teacher of the Year. Following that, I was honored at the state level with the Kohl Foundation Fellowship Excellence in Teaching award. I was making a difference, yet inside I was deeply depressed and despondent about life in general.

Over the last few years, I had gone to counseling, Al-Anon, had been on anti-depressants and even seriously considered ending my life. Overall, I felt dead inside and didn't know how to get out of it. I didn't know, any more than my students did in that moment, what I would do if I knew I couldn't fail because I still felt like a failure. But, somehow I knew there *must be* something more than all of this, and I kept asking Spirit to show me a new way.

Later, a dear friend called, chattering excitedly about a Reiki I class she had just attended over the weekend. Tana was sharing her amazing Spiritual experience, and I was trying my best to connect with what she was telling me, but I had no reference point. Suddenly, she was inviting me to a Reiki I class at her home in a few weeks. Would I come? I hesitated, as the $200 seemed like a lot of money at the time, and I didn't really understand what it was about. Sensing my indecision, she added softly, "Olivia asked me to invite you. Will you come?"

Olivia is our first child who died at the age of one year and three days in 1991. About two months after her birth, we took her to a pediatric neurologist to find out why the fontanelles (skull plates) in her skull were overlapped.

We thought they would tell us that her brain was growing faster than her skull could expand, that she would just need surgery to correct it. Instead, we were devastated to find out that her brain wasn't growing much at all. It was a year filled with hospital stays, doctors, therapists and insurmountable testing that could never tell us the origin of the problem. Looking back, I realized it was really a year of Olivia teaching us, and everyone who came in contact with her, how to love, without ever saying a word.

Now it was 14 years later and I was still feeling guilt, disappointment and failure – like somehow I could have done more. If I had a message from Olivia, I would honor her request. I said, "YES!"

## My Turning Point

I showed up to the class with a very skeptical attitude. While listening to the Spiritual teachings, I realized that I was holding my emotions under lock and key, burying them deep inside, and it was killing me. All that I knew was to 'talk about it', and that meant dumping it on someone, which left me feeling worse. Writing about 'it' kept me reliving the same stories. Here, I was beginning to feel hopeful as I received the knowledge and tools that could change my life.

The caveat was, I would have to take responsibility for what I was creating!

## Taking stock

At my Turning Point I knew my choices were…

- I could continue as I was, hoping things would somehow change, and I would somehow begin to feel better.
- I could continue to complain and feel sorry for myself, surrounded with empathetic friends who didn't know what to do for me.
- I could commit to this work and actively use the tools to transform those old, stuck feelings into something positive – creating a new, joy-filled, positive life.
- I could take responsibility for what I was creating with my thoughts, words and actions and transform those emotions into a positive way of life.

## Making it happen

'Everything happens for a reason' has always been a mantra that has brought me peace of mind. I decided to honor what I had learned and to commit to working on myself – beginning with what I had learned in the Reiki class. When things in my life weren't going as I had hoped, I looked first to myself – my thoughts, words, actions, and the belief systems that were creating these challenging circumstances. Then I set my intention for what I wanted to create and used what I had learned to work through the issue. The more I did this, the better my days became, and the more my outlook on life changed for the better.

# My plan for improvement

I...

- committed to utilizing the tools and strategies I had learned in my Reiki I class.
- decided to learn even more, reading recommended books and going to workshops that empowered me.
- found energy healers who could help me move through deeper issues and patterns that created blocks in moving forward with my intentions.
- learned how to use my writing to connect with Divine guidance with a focus on solutions rather than problems.
- utilized my gift of writing to create new stories of how I would like things to be.
- found like-minded people for friendship and support – invaluable!
- decided to begin my own business to inspire, heal and motivate people who wanted to make positive changes in their lives.
- invested in learning other modes of energetic healing to broaden my knowledge base, heal my life and assist others who were ready to heal their lives, for example:
    - became certified in Spiritual Response Therapy, building my confidence to heal myself and embrace change.
    - became certified in Reiki II.
    - became a Reiki Master.
    - became certified in the Lifeline Technique.

## Moving forward my way

The old days of feeling disconnected from life are over. I am now free to feel more love, hope and optimism in all areas of my life, as well as motivate others to do the same. I am moving forward and looking forward to publishing more books that will inspire and support others who desire 'something more' in their lives. When faced with a challenge along the way, I now remember the gifts of challenges past, and that this will not last – it is really an opportunity to grow and become more whole. It really is a miracle!

## Wisdom from along the way

I have learned...

- Every experience you have created will serve you to grow forward in gratitude for the lessons and gifts it has contained.
- It is essential to ask for help and allow others to support you.
- Trust your guidance and let go of the outcome.
- Notice and value your gifts, then use them to better your life and the lives of others.
- Use the past as a reference to help you understand the circumstances you want to change, then LET IT GO.
- Be open to new experiences and people, for they may bring miraculous opportunities and connections into your life.

# Resources to rave about

## Books
*The Complete Writings of Florence Scovel Shinn* Florence Scovel Shinn (DeVorss Publications, 2005)

*Angelspeake: How to Talk with Your Angels* Barbara Mark and Trudy Griswold (Simon & Schuster, 1995)

*Loving What Is* Byron Katie (Random House, 2002)

## People
Leni Onkka, <u>www.lenionkka.com</u>, an incredible, supportive energy healer who has helped me in so many ways!

AnnaMaria Casper, annacasper.com, her *Breathing Magic into Forgiveness* CD is instrumental in healing one's past. She has assisted me in moving through my toughest circumstances with grace and love

# FROM PEOPLE PLEASER TO AN IMAGE CONSULTANT ON HER OWN TERMS

## *SUSAN'S STORY*
## *ON THE ROAD TO TESCO*

## *NAME: SUSAN CARTER*

## About me

I have had many and varied jobs including teaching overseas. I originally come from London, and my travels have finally brought me back to the UK where I work with women who have lost their oomph, who feel muted by life. I start by helping my clients improve their wardrobes, and this has a knock-on effect into many other areas of their lives.

I have settled in the north east of England by the seaside, a move I have taken so I can walk on the beach every day. There is freedom in living by the sea. It speaks of adventure and possibilities of life beyond the horizon. That's what I want for my clients too: a life without limits.

**Website:** www.twenty4carat.com
**Email:** tp@suecarter.biz

**Gifts:** Send me an email to receive your FREE ebook and occasional newsletter, all available from my website www.twenty4carat.com

## In the beginning

I liked to think of myself as a nice person. I was considerate, thoughtful and would always try to do my best. A bit like the cub scouts in the packs I had run over the years. I didn't like saying no and was very conscious of what other people thought of me. I was a fully paid up member of the 'what will the neighbours think' brigade. The only thing was that I didn't actually know this. I thought I was brave, free spirited and my own woman. It took a huge knock from life to point out the truth.

I was living in Hong Kong, married with two young children. My husband decided that he wanted a divorce and suddenly I was back in England with the children, my self-esteem in shreds and supply teaching my only source of income. Supply teaching is not great so I trained as an image consultant and started my own business. Why image? Well, I had got into this in Hong Kong. It was the 80s and we all had our colours done. I found that I loved colour and style and the whole idea of helping women with the issues that are currently manifested in their less-than-perfect wardrobes. Unfortunately, back in Staffordshire, it seemed that the women near where I lived didn't share my enthusiasm, and business was less than brisk. It was time to do something about this or return to the classroom.

As the second option was enough to make me break out in a cold sweat, I decided to employ a business coach to help me. I thought I just needed guidance on how to find clients, but it didn't turn out quite like that. The life coach, Annie, had the knack of asking tricky questions; she made me look at myself and my life. At times I wasn't sure I liked what I saw, especially when I looked beyond the surface of my mind and went deeper. It was an email exchange with Annie that led me to change my life. It was one of those emails that you regret sending the moment you press the send button, one of those emails that should never have been written in the first place. I felt bad, felt ashamed of myself for what I had written in that email to Annie. I wanted to take it back. I had judged the other person with no evidence; I was in the wrong. Alas, emails cannot be easily recalled, and I wrote another one to Annie saying how bad I felt. And this is what she replied:

*Anyway, it doesn't matter what I think. It only matters what you think.*

What rot; of course it mattered to me what she thought. Why else would I have sent that second email? I wanted her to think well of me. I didn't want her to know that I was capable of bitchy comments or judging people behind their backs. I wanted Annie to like me! I wanted everyone to like me. I wanted them all to know that I am a nice person. I wanted to be loved! That email irked me all afternoon. It made me think about how I treated people and how I wanted them to treat me. It was the grain of sand in the oyster shell that leads to the pearl.

## My Turning Point

Driving down to Tesco that evening, I was still mulling over Annie's reply. Why did it matter whether my coach liked me or not?

It was halfway there that I got my answer. It did not matter. I was paying her to be my coach. Like or dislike did not come into the equation; we were in a financial relationship and she worked with me no matter what her personal feelings. And if it didn't matter what she thought then maybe, just maybe, it didn't matter what other people thought of me either. In that moment I was free.

---

### Taking stock

At my Turning Point I knew my choices were...

- I cannot please all of the people all of the time. So no more trying.
- 'No' was going to be my 'go to' word from now on.
- I could stop explaining myself to people when I didn't want to fit in with their wishes.
- I was free to live my life my way; after all, I am the person I spend 24/7 with.

---

## Making it happen

Now, I don't want you to think that this insight has changed me into a self-obsessed woman who puts herself first and the rest of the world out the door and round the corner. If anything, it's the opposite. As I settled into this knowledge I noticed how I became more understanding and caring. It was as if stopping worrying what other people thought about me allowed me to see them more clearly. The 'do they like me noise' was gone, and I could listen to them. I finally understood the word 'empathy' and it has actually made me a better person. I am more likeable, more approachable and I like myself a whole lot more too. I still have days when the old feelings pop up, but I just remind myself that what other people think of me is none of my business and they go away.

# My plan for improvement

I...

- did a lot of work on myself, finding Inner Susy. Once I got over the shock of finding her, I worked on listening to and trusting her.
- had a Fashion Feng Shui consultation with Evana Maggiore and then implemented her suggestions. This led to throwing out all my high heeled shoes in a glorious burst of energy.
- built up a wardrobe that only contains clothes I love and adore.
- put my house on the market so that I could make my move to the seaside.
- gifted so much household stuff to make way for my new life.
- went on courses about business and joined a mentoring group.
- sought out a business coach who could help me add some structure to my business.
- learned how to use social networking for my business rather than just checking up on my family.
- vowed to treat my business as a business not just something I do.
- planned to build my client list by various means.
- started writing as much as possible and set up a blog. I find writing touches the part of me that wants to live life to the full.
- looked at how to expand my business so that I can reach as many women as possible by online means. This means ebooks, video, whatever it takes.

## Moving forward my way

My days of people pleasing are far behind me, and I have become the woman I was meant to be. I have so much fun helping other women turn their lives around. My business takes me into their wardrobes and their souls, and they come out the other side stronger and happier.

I am content in my cottage by the sea, and that good feeling is spreading out far and wide in a way I never imagined possible before that run to Tesco.

---

## Wisdom from along the way

I have learned...

- No one needs to wear high heels.
- You do not need ten pairs of black trousers.
- Keeping healthy and fit is a must.
- Don't be afraid to stop and smell the roses.
- Listen to your heart: it knows the answers.
- People want to help, and you just have to ask.
- We all have too much stuff in our wardrobes, houses and minds. Let it go.

# Resources to rave about

**Books**

*The Artist's Way: A Spiritual Path to Higher Creativity* Julia Cameron (Penguin Putman, 2002)

*Steering by Starlight* Martha Beck (Piatkus Books, 2008)

**Web**

Fashion Feng Shui with Evana Maggiore, www.fashionfengshui.com, Fashion Feng Shui does for dressing what Feng Shui does for your home or business. Fashion Feng Shui® teaches you how to dress with mindfulness and intention every day so that what you are wearing expresses who you are at your core and attracts your deepest desires

# FROM DYSLEXIA TO INTERNATIONAL CAREER

## *NICOLE'S STORY*
## *THE SLOW ONE*

## *NAME: NICOLE D LE MAIRE*

## About me

A single, Dutch energetic, resourceful and dynamic HR consultant with extensive experience across a broad range of HR functions, I founded my company, Human Resources Global Limited, at the age of 34. For the last 12 years I have worked for many blue chip organisations, taking responsibility for all areas of international Human Resources in various countries as part of my global HR responsibilities. I manage Human Resources Global Limited with a highly skilled and specialist team who work for me on a regular basis.

After working and living in more countries than anyone I know and loving every minute of it  − being integrated with the culture, traditions and people − I have obtained so many interesting and valuable experiences across the world in both my career in Human Resources and my personal life.

**Website:**  www.humanresourcesglobal.com
**Email:**    nicole@humanresourcesglobal.com

**Gift:** Human Resources Global Ltd. "Thinking Global, Acting Local". I draw on 12 years of experience working on international Human Resources subjects and issues. I offer **a free, no-obligation 45-minute consultation** to assist and help you and your organisation to begin the process of analysing your needs in order to advise you on how Human Resources Global Ltd. might be able to help you. Email me for more details.

## In the beginning

*"I, myself, was always recognised.... as the 'slow one' in the family. It was quite true, and I knew it and accepted it. Writing and spelling were always terribly difficult for me. My letters were without originality. I was... an extraordinarily bad speller and have remained so until this day."*
*- Agatha Christie*

Have u ever read a gape and not kombleteli understoed wat it sad… Have u witten a word uzing totalli differnt letters and tuning letters arownd? It is a little like learning a new language everyday…

Even without a formal diagnosis, I understood early on (at age two to three) that I was different; I have come a long way from the 'dumb', 'stupid', 'lazy' labels that were part of my primary and secondary school experience.

No one at work or in my personal life other than my family has known about my dyslexia – until now! I was and still am 'afraid' that it will go against me in my personal and work life.

It is often said that dyslexic children are extra creative; however, I think dyslexia lends itself to a different way of thinking and doing. Always thinking outside the box – as this is the way my brain functions – can actually make it quite difficult to write something in an organised manner.

Living in a very nice suburb in Rotterdam, a big port city, with my parents and two older brothers and a younger sister, I guess I was always the one who was just not quite so bright. My family is very clever and they all went to university in Holland, but in secondary school my parents were told that I was '*dom*' and would never be able to go to university – I would go to the lowest level school available and work in a shop.

"They're ruining my life! The school doesn't even know what I can do," I told my parents. They, of course, did not agree with the school's assessment and I was sent to a small high school where I was given extra time and attention which was helpful. Because my dyslexia did not affect me, it gave me the confidence to go further in life.

My language grades were terrible in the first years of high school – until I knew that I was going to go to the USA, that is. Then suddenly my English grades went up from Ds to As in two short months. Amazing what motivation and enthusiasm can do!

At 16 years of age I wanted to spend a year in the USA on a high school exchange. I thought it would be the best way to leave Holland and all the negative school experiences behind me. I knew 100 per cent for sure that I would love it. I would be able to live on my own, without people always saying, "Can you do this?" or "Can you do that?"

My mother saved up for me to go on this exchange, as she knew that it would be very good for my future. I applied to a well-known exchange organisation (EF), but was not allowed to go to the US, as I was judged to be too shy and lacking in confidence (real dyslexia traits). They were afraid that I would not be able to live without my family. Me? Unable to live without my family? The USA at that time did actually have phones and computers...

## My Turning Point

I have never been so mad in my life at a dream not coming true. After another "NO, you cannot go on a US exchange", I told my mum, "I will go to the US and no one will stop me". As many people know, another dyslexia trait is stubbornness and total determination!

So I had the choice to give up... or to be determined and apply to more US exchange organisations. Well, I am not a 'giving upper' (the dyslexia term) and knew I would go to the US; I didn't even think that I wouldn't go there.

## Taking stock

At my Turning Point I knew my choices were…

- I could work hard where I was.
- I could give up.
- I could have a sense of persistence and follow my plan.

## Making it happen

I wrote to other exchange organisations. They said, "As you're so determined – you have already achieved your year."

So I went to the US at 16 to live with a family in Nebraska. I had no problem with my dyslexia! I had the best English grade in the class: me – a Dutch girl with dyslexia! It was the best decision I ever made. Definitely the best time of my life...

This is not a Turning Point showing how I overcame my struggles, but the story of coming a long way by walking the talk, demonstrating that with positive decisions and helping others, everyone with dyslexia can do the same. I realised that, along with weaknesses, I also had strengths – not just stubbornness and determination!

My passion is to develop and stimulate people; although I have dyslexia, I can still wear a business suit and achieve things professionally.

# My plan for improvement

I...

- worked harder and longer than anyone during my teenage years and twenties, using every strategy I could find to successfully pass my exams, finding ways that no one knew existed in terms of studying, and receiving merits and distinctions for all my diplomas, a BA, a MA HRM and even a MBA. It was every bit as hard as I knew it would be; it meant working long hours and sticking with it – YET, I did it my way!
- went to study in Scotland and England, as I did not feel like Holland was 'my country', due to my dyslexia in Dutch. (A psychologist I once chatted to in a professional women's club said that my feeling of being uncomfortable in Holland was due to a traumatic childhood. It would have been good to see my parents' faces at this. Me? A traumatic childhood just because of my dyslexia? Very funny!) I knew my English was a lot better than my mother tongue... AND although I do not have a US or British passport, I probably belong there more than in my native country. Perhaps this is another challenge for the future...
- I decided I would:
    - travel more.
    - network.
    - help children with dyslexia.
    - be positive in my behaviour and thinking.

## Moving forward my way

I learned the only way to manage dyslexia is to work *with*, not against, it.

I have had many choices: to be the person others wanted me to be or become who I wanted to be; wondering why I never achieved my dreams, or using my dyslexia to improve my survival strategies and my drive to achieve what I really want from life.

Dyslexia and people not believing in me did not stop me from reaching my dreams, as I now have my own business. I even studied Arabic, using my dyslexia as a positive tool in my life – not so 'slow' now!

---

## Wisdom from along the way

I have learned…

- Respect your individuality.
- Cultivate a stubbornness, a determination to achieve what you want.
- Never ever, ever give up.
- Set goals for success.
- Use your intuition.
- Remember: One door closes and many others open...

# Resources to rave about

## Organisations
Aspect Foundation, www.aspectfoundation.org,
the organisation that did allow me on my exchange

Soroptomists International,
www.soroptimistinternational.org, the organisation for
women across the world

The linked-in group which I manage and started,
Human Resources Global: Inspiring Global Women
http://www.linkedin.com

# FROM TERRORIST ATTACK AT THE PENTAGON TO COMPLETE LIFE CHANGE

## LINDA'S STORY
## RECOGNIZING YOUR TURNING POINT AND FINDING YOUR PATH

## NAME: LINDA A JANSSEN

## About me

Mine is a story about continual growth, identifying your truest passions, taking risks and ultimately, reinvention. In a previous life, I was a senior foreign affairs specialist with the US Department of Defense, working on sensitive national security and defense policy issues. I left Washington, DC for North Carolina in 2004, and eventually moved to The Netherlands. Rejecting the label of 'trailing spouse' (as if I were bougainvillea trailing along a garden trellis!), I chose instead to recognize this move as the gift that it was: an opportunity to redefine myself. Today I'm a freelance writer, aspiring author, and have recently launched my boldest endeavor to date. I now live with my family in The Hague.

**Website:** www.adventuresinexpatland.com
www.voicesabroadproject.com
**Email:** linda@adventuresinexpatland.com
linda@voicesabroadproject.com

**Gift:** If you sign up to receive my monthly newsletter, I'll also send you a free guide 'Live Your Best Expat Life'. Details available at my website www.adventuresinexpatland.com.

## In the beginning

Growing up in a rural town in up-state New York, there was little to suggest a career and life in the international arena. Yet from the moment I discovered the news weekly *Time* magazine as an 11-year-old, I was hooked. Reading about the political, economic, cultural or foreign policy dimensions of various issues, I dreamed of traveling and working in exotic locales. I also loved to write, and from an early age I enjoyed weaving stories in my head, occasionally capturing them on the page.

Once, while attending a friend's birthday party, I recall her mother plopping on the table a pile of school newspapers written two years prior. We spent the next half hour regaling each other with our amateurish attempts at journalism. One humorous story I'd written about a failed family camping trip caught my eye. Skimming the page, I was pleasantly surprised by what I read. I'd completely forgotten contributing to the class newspaper, but my enjoyment in reading the hilarious misadventures involving a woefully leaning tent, long queues for showers and the pathetic absence of wilderness skills left me wondering why. *This isn't that bad*, I mused. The words still had the ability to make me laugh.

In the ensuing years, school work and activities took precedence. My interest in international issues grew, and writing receded into the background. It never even occurred to me that I might study writing as a career choice.

*If everyone has to write as a student*, I reasoned, *how incredibly difficult must it be to write well enough to support yourself in a paying job?* And writing a book? Impossible.

Looking up international relations careers in the archaic job description cards of my high school guidance office, I found only 'interpreter/translator'. But I knew even then that there was so much more out there in the world beyond deciphering someone else's words, and I fully intended to find it.

I studied international relations in college and graduate school, moved to Washington and began my career. I met and married my husband, Daniel; he had also pursued degrees in international affairs and been an expat during his teen years. We loved to travel, and spoke longingly of one day moving abroad to share with our future children the definitive experiences that living in another culture had provided him.

As our careers took hold and the promotions came, the dream of living in a foreign country faded into the background. With two young children and success in our respective careers, it never seemed the right time to consider uprooting our family to head overseas. Writing was integral to my professional work, yet only rarely did I put pen to paper for personal writing projects.

Back at the Pentagon in June 2001 after a nine-month, senior-level program with our US State Department, I became a director in the newly established territorial security group in the Under Secretary of Defense for Policy's office. I was to lead a small team of military and civilian personnel responsible for policy support regarding chemical, biological, radiological, nuclear or high-yield explosive events at home and overseas.

## My Turning Point

America was under attack. As the combating terrorism policy crisis team finished an emergency meeting at 9:37 am, the building shook violently. A rumbling roar, akin to a freight train, tore through the room. We realized immediately what had occurred.

*I've survived*, I thought, stunned. *A plane has hit the Pentagon, and I'm still alive.*

Rushing into the corridor, we met the approaching wall of thick, black, acrid smoke, the pungent smell of burning jet fuel. I later learned the plane's nose wheel came to rest less than 30 feet away; I'd also lost two colleagues. Life would never, no, *could never* be the same.

## Taking stock

At my Turning Point I knew my choices were…

- I was reminded in graphic, unequivocal terms that our time on this earth is finite and precious.
- This wasn't about death and dying; this was about life and living.
- In the immediate aftermath of September 11th, I felt personally and professionally committed to staying put, at least for the time being. I owed my country as much.
- As time passed and the immediacy of the events receded, I faced a major decision.
- I could continue working in this fast-paced environment, becoming more removed from direct international work with each new assignment and fighting burnout.
- Or I could make a radical change in lifestyle and location, identify what I truly wanted to do in life, and take the leap.

## Making it happen

The surety that I was doing what I was destined to do was missing. Reflection helped confirm my true passions: writing and the international arena. But how to integrate them? In the absence of a clear-cut plan, I trusted my instincts. I had faith that I would discover the answers so long as I remained open to new experiences, acquired new skills, was attuned to opportunities, and sought change that brought me closer to my passions.

Moving outside the Washington, DC area afforded a much needed 'career detox' and better work-life balance. I found contract work supporting an international research company. I began writing again, but struggled. My husband was offered a great job in The Hague, and we leapt at the chance. Pieces of the puzzle were falling into place. Living abroad offered a great opportunity for reinvention. I just needed to fill in the missing pieces.

## My plan for improvement

I...

- took stock of my skill set, determining I needed to learn more on both the creative and business sides of writing (for example, freelancing, copywriting, content marketing, blogging, search engine optimization).
- completed courses in freelance writing, blogging and social media, creative writing.
- developed a one-year strategic plan for my writing career, then fleshed out comprehensive sub-plans for different aspects.
- designed and launched my website, steadily building readership for my award-winning expat blog.
- performed industry, market and site analysis to identify and exploit potential opportunities for publication and brand expansion.
- built a portfolio of published work, then transitioned to commissioned work augmented with strategically placed gratis work that builds traffic and name-recognition.
- began growing local and global networks to expand my body of published work, generate new projects, grow my 'brand'.

- developed a network of similarly serious writers, helping to form a writers' group committed to critical feedback and honing our craft.
- invested in coaching, specifically targeting key challenges impeding progress.
- conceived and launched a second website to showcase the stories, in their own words, of individuals abroad.

## Moving forward my way

Overcoming writing inhibitions proved key to unleashing my creative self. I focus on my niche: chronicling aspects of life abroad, exploring expat issues, helping current or hopeful expats. In addition to my blog, articles and a regular expat website gig, I run the Voices Abroad Project and am under contract for a related book. I'm writing a book on emotional resilience, plus my memoir and a first novel. Each day I wake energized, and go to sleep with ideas bouncing around my head. In melding my true passions, I honor myself.

## Wisdom from along the way

I have learned…

- Don't waste time, energy, or effort resisting change; revel in it! At the very least, make peace with it.
- Doing what you're passionate about doesn't feel like work; it's energizing.
- Do your research. Focus on your 'brand' to do the right things at the right time for the right reasons.
- Dream big. If you visualize it, you can articulate it.

- No plan is static. As you implement, evaluate and adjust.
- Cast your net far and wide. Be open to the opportunities and success that may come from unexpected sources
- Deliver as promised, but don't over promise. Avoid spreading yourself becoming overwhelmed.
- Embrace the adage 'you learn something new every day'. Better yet, learn three or four!

## Resources to rave about

**Books**

*What Should I Do With My Life?: The True Story of People Who Answered the Ultimate Question* Po Bronson (Ballantine Books 2005)

*The Artist's Way: A Spiritual Path to Higher Creativity* Julia Cameron (Penguin Putman, 2002)

**Web**

Write to done, www.writetodone.com, www.writersdigest.com useful tips to hone your writing skills in all genres

Copy blogger, www.copyblogger.com, strategies & insights for bloggers, copywriters, content marketers, freelancers.

Seth Godin, www.sethgodin.com, strategies & insights for bloggers, copywriters, content marketers, freelancers.

**People**

Jo Parfitt, www.joparfitt.com, lives her motto 'sharing what I know to help others to grow' and helps others to achieve their writing dreams

# FROM DREAM TO REALITY

## *ANNA'S STORY*
## *THINKING OF OTHERS AND NOT MYSELF*

She challenged herself to do more with her life to bring health and financial stability for the benefit of others, rather than to be centred on her own interest and pleasure.

## *NAME: ANNA KOKUEVA*

## About me
My story shows that a well-organized and easy life of a young expatriate was no longer enough for me to be happy and feel myself complete. I searched for additional ways of utilising my resources for the benefit of the well-being of my family and friends. Originally from Yaroslavl, a city on the Northeast of Moscow, I have studied and lived in Russia, Finland and France and been based in Paris

since 2007. With four years of international experience in project management and business analysis, I was selected as having high potential by the age of 24. I joined a big multinational, Air Liquide, one of the Global Fortune 500, right after my graduation from Sciences Po Paris. I take my inspiration both from nature and from people who made significant achievements. While being active, working, running or walking along the banks of the Seine, new ideas mature in my mind.

**Website:** www.agel.com
**Email:** anna.kokueva@gmail.com

## In the beginning

Young, enthusiastic and result-driven, in my daily work I combined analytical, consulting and team missions. I had significant freedom of action and many things to learn in my work. My secure job and expatriate position allowed me to have an easy and relaxed lifestyle in the heart of cosmopolitan Paris. This was exactly the work and life I had dreamt of since I was a teenager.

When my working day was finished, my social activities and exchanges were just getting started. As a welcomed participant at all major events, from political and business clubs to sports and fashion weeks, I had become truly adept at the Parisian lifestyle and a master of French traditions and etiquette.

It was a sunny day in late April. I was working on the computer in my office in La Defense in Paris when, suddenly, a strange feeling came over me; I felt as if I was slipping into a trance. I tried to concentrate on my work, but

I could hardly focus on what I was doing. My imagination took me far away from that business environment. I asked myself: "What does my life stand for? What is my mission? How would I like to be remembered forever?"

After a couple of carefree years in Paris, challenged by these questions, my imagination changed direction and the next minute it brought me back to my hometown. I returned to the foundations of my inner self, my Russian origins and Slavic soul, and to the values I have acquired from my family. Naturally concerned about people around me, I understood that I could not stay self-centred any longer. I needed to embrace a vaster human perimeter and to share my knowledge, experience and provide my support to those who needed it.

But what about those I cared for? Working hard, putting in long hours and travelling extensively, my mother hardly complained about anything. However, she had recently mentioned that her health was getting fragile. At that time, I did not take it seriously, but now I realised that my work and activities would be useless unless I could find a solution to help the person that I loved the most. Tears filled my eyes, and I went out to take some air.

It was no longer possible to continue living solely for my own interest and pleasure. I thought that if I did not make an effort to change my life today and start finding a solution to help my mother feel better, than I would lose the moment, and a feeling of regret would remain in my heart for the rest of my life.

One day a good acquaintance suggested I attend a presentation about his new revolutionary business. Very curious to know the details of this adventure, I did not have any special expectations, and went to the meeting keeping my mind free to discover a very new concept.

## My Turning Point

"You are at the right place at the right time. You have a chance to join the company at the creation phase just before its vast expansion. It is an ideal moment to invest in this business since 70 percent of wealth is created at this stage." I can still hear the speaker's voice that convinced me, even several months after this presentation. Being in charge of analysis of the business models and growth strategies in my job, I acquired necessary analytical and synthetic skills that allowed me to capture the urgency of the moment and the importance of my decision. As I have recognized that I was being given a chance, I decided to act immediately and I joined this business as an investor.

---

### Taking stock

At my Turning Point I knew my choices were…

- I could easily continue living and working as I did before by taking advantage of my young expatriate life without asking too many questions.
- I could deny an opportunity to face new challenges, learn new skills and meet active and interesting people on my way.
- Having an initial interest in this new activity, I could also keep a passive position without taking any concrete actions.
- I might also say that it was too risky, time-consuming or just expensive for me.

# Making it happen

I carefully examined each piece of information about the company's technology, patents, finances, management and its international recognition. I was amazed that my personal mission had so much in common with Agel's one that is about to improve the quality of life of millions around the world.

After a month of research, I was convinced that Agel's invention based on a gel suspension technology would help millions be healthier due to the highest bioavailability and nutritional efficiency of vitamins in a gel form. It will also push the whole market further technologically and replace vitamins in form of pills and tablets. World athletes, a sensitive consumer group in the nutrition market, became its early followers.

I decided to participate in the Agel's next international event that took place in Moscow and I went there to meet and learn from the top leaders. Afterwards, driving to my family house I was excited to share this opportunity with my family members that could have helped them solving health problems and diversifying revenue streams.

## My plan for improvement

I...

- imposed on myself a certain discipline in terms of physical activities and life planning. I started to use the product on the daily basis, I scheduled my sports activities three times per week and began to write down daily, weekly and monthly plans that helped me to be more efficient and organised.

- read most of the relevant literature about the company, wellness industry and its perspectives in English, French and Russian.
- invested in learning materials and working tools. I bought books, mp3 recordings and used every spare minute to learn whether I was commuting, running or at home.
- attended local and international training events. I approached unknown people, asked questions and shared knowledge. In Russia, I took the chance to tell my story and share my objectives in front of 2000 people.
- kept in close contact with the person who had invited me to join this project. I expanded my network and met wonderful and very efficient people from various backgrounds and countries that I could have hardly met elsewhere. They were a source of help and inspiration.
- started to coach high potentials in Russia in two sessions of two to three hours per week. As my team was not able to learn in English, I suggested they use the synthesis of 'best practices' that I had drawn up from my English materials.
- realised that I would not be able to go to Russia to support my business there, so I decided to work with a strong local leader, preferring to share the revenues with her than condemn my business and team to a slow growth.

# Moving forward my way

My past dissatisfaction is over. New skills that I have learnt from working with Agel have brought a sense of joy and meaning to my life; they have also helped me to recharge my motivation levels and interest in my corporate job. Four months after starting using the product, my parents have not only managed to solve several health problems, they have also created a source of constant residual income. In six months the Russian organization has developed to about 100 people, and is growing unceasingly. To tell the truth, people believe that my mother is 20 years younger than her biological age.

## Wisdom from along the way

I have learned…

- The best way to predict the future is to invent it.
- Keep chasing your dream.
- For things to change, *you* have to change.
- Nothing works unless I do.
- Work more on yourself and invest more in your personal education, than you would work on your job or business.
- When you are not able to implement your ideas by yourself, call for a partner; it is better to go faster together, then slowly on one's own way.
- Serving others sincerely, I feel that my life has meaning and importance. Seeing the results in people that I help brings me joy and satisfaction and keeps me on track, even in very hard times.

- It is better to fail at climbing the mountain of your dreams, than to regret a chance or an opportunity that you rejected without even trying it; just like when you set your target too low, and you quickly overcome your limits.
- Try to treat losses and difficulties as the best learning experience that helps you acquire new skills. We learn significantly more by losing than when do on the winning path.
- The sun always shines after the dark night. Keep yourself in action, stay connected with your friends and do not stop helping those who truly need you.

## Resources to rave about

**Books**

*The New Wellness Revolution* Paul Zane Pilzer
(Wiley, 2002)

*The Next Millionaires* Paul Zane Pilzer
(Momentum media, 2005)

*Think and Grow Ric,* Napoleon Hill
(Jeremy P. Tatcher / Penguin, 2005)

*How to Win Friends and Influence People* Dale Carnegie
(Vermilion, 1981)

*The Treasury of Quotes* Jim Rohn (Jim Rohn International, 2006)

*Leading an Inspired Life* Jim Rohn
(Nightingale Conant, 1996)

# FROM IDENTITY CRISIS TO COACHING THROUGH ART

## *NATALIE'S STORY*
## *WHAT DOES MOSAIC HAVE TO DO WITH THIS?*

## *NAME: NATALIE TOLLENAERE*

## About me
In September 2003 we arrived in South Africa. My ninth move in 20 years, with four children and one husband. I have lived in eight different countries (Morocco, India, Guinea-Bissau, Germany, Zambia, South Africa, Rwanda and Belgium, my home country). Grabbing job opportunities as we moved, my career is a mosaic: building a school in a village in Zambia, running an art gallery, creating an art school, running a chicken farm, selling waffles at markets to manage the month end, running canteens in three

different schools, being responsible for the famine relief programme in Zambia... besides being a full-time mother and wife. As you can perceive, I'm a creative person... but September 2003 took me by surprise...

**Website:** www.transitionstoafrica.com
**Email:** natalie.toll@gmail.com

> **Gift:** 45-minute phone coaching session for accompanying spouses wanting to create a life from the challenges of their expatriation. To receive this, send me an email with the title "Turning Points".

## In the beginning

I'm sitting on a box. My body feels like a potato bag. The smell of cardboard coming from the unpacked boxes makes me feel nauseous. Where do I start? What do I have to do next? I send an SMS to my friend in Zambia: "Got the container. What should I do next? HELP!" Tears are rolling down my cheeks and I promise myself that I will never move again. Packing, unpacking, finding the shops, finding new friends, getting used to a new culture, new language, never again...

I am what is commonly called a 'trailing spouse' which means that I follow my husband wherever in the world he is posted. This means that I'm 'the wife of the doctor', 'the wife of Mr Tihon'. It is even worse when people ask me what I do in life. I have two choices: I can either tell them the truth: "I'm a housewife and a trailing spouse", which has an immediate effect on them − "Ah"

– and before I can try to tell them more about me I find myself alone and them speaking to my husband about important things. Or I can tell them: "I'm an expert in packing". This has another immediate effect – "Oh" – with a smile (of pity) and still they go off to far more interesting adult conversations.

My landing in South Africa was rough. My position as a trailing spouse was weighing on my shoulders. Yes, it gave me the opportunity to explore the world, to raise four children who had turned out to be real nice kids, to build a relationship that was stable enough to put up with every move. I had built around me a world of stability in my unstable life. I had built a shield around myself to prevent the stress of the expatriate life from touching me. But on my arrival in South Africa, the shield started to show signs of wearing out. My inner world started being touched by the 'weight of the boxes'. I became very fragile.

I realized that although I knew THE world (or part of the world), I didn't know MY world.

I did manage to unpack the full household for six people, and make the house look like a home again. I painted the walls in warm colours that made me feel at home, hung the pictures, planted flowers in the garden, became familiar with the shopping malls, even made some connections with people... but then what? What would I do now with my life, transplanted in South Africa? I had no idea. I was as empty as my boxes...

So I became 'the wife of Dr Tihon', but this time we could add 'depressed'. I was shutting myself up inside my packing boxes. Ignoring the world around me, fearing it, feeling tired, feeling fragile, feeling out of place like a fish out of the pond, I just wanted to be alone in my box!

But what does one do alone in a box? I had nothing to do, but explore MY world... and this is exactly where my career started.

## My Turning Point

A voice inside me or inside the box (I'm not sure if boxes talk or not!) was telling me to do things I really wanted to do. Things that I had always wanted to do but never had (or took!) time to.

I was flipping through the little Jobourg-acceuil booklet, thinking: what can these people do for me anyway? My eye caught an advert for a one-day mosaic class. It took a lot of strength for me to pick up my phone and call the lady.

That phone call was the beginning of my career.

---

### Taking stock

At my Turning Point I knew my choices were...

- Sulk, sulk and sulk.
- Over-protecting my children, become over-involved in their homework and school stuff, be on their backs all the time (that could have been a full-time job – but unpaid!).
- Close myself up and retire into my inner world, sealing the box, forever with tape.
- Being over-social with anybody and losing myself in it. (I had done that before!)
- Take this opportunity to find my direction in life.

---

## Making it happen

After the first mosaic class, I bought myself a small table and painted it sky blue, maybe already unconsciously hoping that this table would lead me to my dream. I started doing mosaic work. As soon as the kids had gone to school (which was as early as 6.30am) till they came back I did mosaic work. I used tiles, broken glass, paper, melted glasses, egg shells, wires, broken plates, cups, beads, and ended up creating my own tassels with clay. From small items like boxes (yes, of course, boxes!) I advanced to tables and then big tables. I carried on for about two years...

The process of putting all these pieces together brought me back to the reality of my own life. As a metaphor, I was putting all the pieces of my life together. I was creating my own life 'artwork'.

### My plan for improvement

In mosaic, I could create from perfectly shaped pieces to broken and unshaped pieces. It helped me to realize that, in life, I could do the same. I could create from good and perfect events as well as from bad and disastrous events. I could also leave some pieces behind. It was up to me, it was my choice. Here is what I did:

I...

- created a CV of my life history: I called it my 'life journey'. I wrote down every single thing I had done, including the deliveries of my children, the packing and unpacking, the jobs... I presented it like a CV. This CV helped me discover the following:

- I discovered what I was worth and that I was very skilled.
- I discovered that my life experience could benefit me and others.
- I discovered that I could build up a business based on all these experiences.
- I decided that if I open up, life will open up to me.
- I decided to listen, look and take opportunities.
- I realized that, to give me some confidence, I needed some formal training.

## Moving forward my way

Magically, coming out of my box, I started meeting the right people at the right time. The wonderful Johannes and Min Fidler both told me: "Never doubt that you are an artist." I returned to my first love: ceramic art.

Andrea introduced me to art therapy. As I trained I used art to process emotions. Jo Parfitt introduced me to the specificity of the expatriate community. Are we different? Why?

And with Donna Carpenter PhD I brought these skills together into a single approach: "The Art of Coaching through Art"©, giving back these skills to the globally mobile community in Africa.

# Wisdom from along the way

I have learned...

- There is always an opportunity behind a challenge.
- Even the most insignificant moment can be significant.
- We always have a choice. Even not choosing is a choice.
- Listening and building up compassion is a life-saving tool.
- Allow yourself to be a beginner. Ask questions.
- Ask for help. There is nothing wrong with that. You actually give a chance to others to be useful. They will love it.
- "Your life is an artwork, you are the artist." Use your creativity in every corner of your life.

# Resources to rave about

**Books**

*The Artist's Way: A Spiritual Path to Higher Creativity*
Julia Cameron (Penguin Putman, 2002)

*You Can Heal Your Life* Louise L. Hay
(Palace Press International, 1999)

*Gift from the Sea* Anne Morrow Lindbergh
(Pantheon Books, 1975)

*Third Culture Kids: The Experience of Growing up
Among Worlds* David Pollock and Ruth Van Reken
(Nicholas Brealey Publishing, 2010)

**People**
Min Fidler, www.applegreenmachine.co.uk

Jo Parfitt, www.joparfitt.com

# FROM FEARFUL TO FEARLESS

## *LORI'S STORY*
## *BRAVING THE TEMPEST AND STEPPING INTO THE LIGHT*

## *NAME: LORI ELGIN*

## About me

By the grace of God, often in utter desperation, and by sheer determination, like the Phoenix I have risen from the ashes of my life more times than I can count. I am a triple board certified nurse practitioner practicing high risk pediatrics. I am an educator, mentor, mom, grandmother, woman of great faith, perpetual student, and natural born traveler. Using keen intuition and deep listening, I empower others to find their unique calling and purpose. I am passionate about coaching those seeking to master their own health and wellness and discover and share their exquisite gifts with the world. To this end, I founded Take the Leap Coaching to combine my gifts, talents, and intuition to allow my clients to discover their own truth, often hidden or disguised deep within.

**Website:** www.LoriElgin.com
**Email:** lori@LoriElgin.com

**Gifts:** Free 45-minute coaching session by telephone or in person, if geography permits. An exciting newsletter combining health, wellness, personal development, parenting, and the love and passion for a life lived to its utmost. To receive the offer, email Lori@LoriElgin.com.

## In the beginning

I grew up an untimely, rather inconvenient child. My earliest memories were of being stuck on the outside and trying to get in. I longed for my parents' love and would change, say, or do anything to be accepted. I knew I was not loved, but I translated this in my young mind to 'I am not lovable', believing in my little heart that no one would ever love me if they knew me. I sought a safe haven and discovered it deep inside myself. Here I could hide and be safe so I withdrew into my cave with its reinforced walls, locks, and heavily shuttered door.

I grew up with a deep paralyzing fear of rejection and an underlying yearning for love and acceptance. This fear crippled me in so many ways. My need to take care of everyone and take on their burdens was merely an outward manifestation, perfectly acceptable in my faith circles.

I disguised and hid my fear, enveloped it, and stuffed it deep within. Yet, all the while, there was a screaming voice in my head in every new situation saying, "Do not go there, Lori; if you do they will reject you. You do not belong here." So I changed, like a chameleon.

This fear tormented me for 60 long years. It was the driving force behind my prolonged disastrous first marriage. I poured my life, energy and passion into my beautiful gifted children. Despite my fear, I finally found the courage to leave. I excelled in nursing school, completing undergraduate, graduate, and post-graduate education and degrees. I thrived in academia. When I became a nurse practitioner, I entered the world I was created for. Here all my gifts, talents, knowledge, faith, and dreams came together. I loved caring for the tiniest, weakest, and sickest babies in five American states. The puzzle of figuring out what was wrong, the never-ending battle with disease and death, the long stress-filled hours, the helping parents to love and oft times let go of their precious babies – this was my world. I became an exceptionally skilled practitioner.

To share my knowledge, I became a teacher. I accepted new and challenging positions, growing, moving and expanding my scope of practice to include pediatrics and family practice. The unique set of skills and talents provided the bridge to my current independent position in high-risk pediatrics for a local hospital. At the pinnacle of my career, with the world's best physicians and staff, we changed the face of newborn care, raised the bar of excellence, providing family-centered, evidence-based medicine.

I met and married a gentle wonderful man who only longed for us to share our lives. We built a beautiful life together. In the midst of my success persisted my deep internal fear. I could overrule it and be a powerful advocate for my patients, family, or friends. But it nagged me, nipping at my soul like a deranged terrier. I always choked when anything turned the spotlight on me, preferring the shadows where I was safe.

Having met all my professional goals, I yearned to make a deeper impact on our world. I hired a coach, learned to nurture and nourish my body, and sought new direction. I turned the spotlight on myself and began to really listen and deal with the issues in my life. I discovered my personal values, set goals, and allowed the vision for my life to unfold. Realizing I had been a coach my entire life, I entered the Morning Coach transformational coaching program.

## My Turning Point

During a session of Tara Marino's 'Beauty Formula', Tara shared Lance Armstrong's definition of fear of rejection. It pierced the darkness where I hide. Looking at the monster that had paralyzed me my entire life, I understood that when I allow fear of others to stop me from speaking, doing, or living my truth, I reject myself. A lifetime of this was the deepest and most painful rejection of all. It was also the ultimate betrayal.

Shaking from the top of my head to the soles of my feet, my stomach churned and my mouth was as dry as cotton. I was reduced to tears.

## Taking stock

At my Turning Point I knew my choices were…

- I could turn off the light. I could hide, cover this up, ignore the truth – very tempting because I had mastered the shadowland for so long.
- But, I knew if I chose to stay here I would die. Maybe not physically but slowly I would dry up and blow away.
- I could step into the roaring tempest of fear, taste the bilious acid, feel the raging torrent, and choose to find myself in the light.
- I could choose to do some serious work on myself.

## Making it happen

Taking a deep breath, I turned around, looked my deepest fear in the eye and stepped headlong into the tempest. I loosed my safety net. I told myself the fear of others' rejection is not more important than accepting myself. "It is time," I said more bravely than I felt.

Realizing I needed to heal the past, I wrote a long letter forgiving my mother. I poured out my heart. Then, when totally spent, I shredded the letter. As the shredder stopped, I felt something shift deep inside me. I felt a powerful, life changing, release of energy. The truth had set me free.

## My plan for improvement

I…

- chose to stand up, and say yes to me, to love and accept myself on an entirely new and different level.
- sat down and journaled. I closely examined how rejection showed up in my life and when the fear first manifested itself.
- stopped and asked myself:
- how do I see myself moving past fear of rejection?
- how will letting go of this fear and my safety zone transform my life?
- what if I allowed myself to face my fear head on and step into my own personal power?
- would I speak my truth and do what I believe is right despite my ever present fear?
- what was I willing to let go of to be sure fear of rejection no longer controlled my life?
- could I give up my buffer space?
- would I really stand up for me?
- realized that all the education, training, and experiences of my life – the good, the bad, the ugly – came together here as the perfect preparation for the new life of transformational coaching.
- founded Take the Leap Coaching as a credentialed life coach.
- began working with the most amazing clients, listening deeply and dancing in the moment with them, allowing them to find their own answers deep within. I had entered into my fullness.
- worked towards completion of my Morning Coach Professional Coaching credentialing.
- pursued Morning Coach Master Coaching and International Coaching Federation credentialing.

## Moving forward my way

I spent 60 years trapped in lies and fear, hidden behind smoke screens, locked in the midst of the tempest. Every event in my life led up to my newest expansion. Now I walk in the light in the middle of the road, on my path, as the shining light I was sent here to be. This past week, I ignored my pounding heart, and with wavering voice and tears I refused to shed, I stood up for me before the most powerful people in my world. I did not give up. I did not hide, but spoke my truth.

## Wisdom from along the way

I have learned…

- Be aware of rejection and how it shows up in your life.
- Consider whose approval you are seeking.
- You need to ask yourself how you are rejecting yourself and your truth.
- Fear is a liar and a thief. By facing it head on, it scatters.
- Ignore the lump in your throat, your pounding pulse, and sweaty palms.
- Get out of your own way.
- Choose you!!
- Let go of fear and your limiting belief.
- Take the leap.
- Live your truth – be you!

# Resources to rave about

**Books**
*Radical Honesty* Brad Blanton (Sounds True Inc, 2005)

*Boundaries: When to Say Yes, How to Say No* Dr Henry
Cloud & John Townsend   (Zondervan, 1992)

*The Big Leap: Conquer Your Hidden Fear and Take Life
to the Next Level* Gay Hendricks (HarperOne, 2010)

**Web**
MorningCoach Podcast JB Glossinger,
www.Morningcoach.com, and iTunes

The Beauty Formula Tara Marino,
www.ElegantFemme.com

**People**
Lance Armstrong,
www.LiveStrong.com

# FROM LOSS OF SELF TO A NEW IDENTITY AS A WRITER

## *SARAH'S STORY*
## *NEVER TOO LATE TO GET STARTED*

## *NAME: SARAH KOBLOW*

## About me

I was born in North Yorkshire, England in 1964, the second eldest of six girls. I have lived in Bahrain, Qatar, France and Holland, while raising my family (Beth 16, Alice 13, and Jonny 11). My first career was social work but travelling has given me opportunities to develop more entrepreneurial means of earning an income. I have been a counsellor and swimming teacher in the Middle East and now a budding writer in The Hague. My rollercoaster life, including successfully surviving childhood abuse, cancer and traumatic bereavement, has helped me learn to truly savour sunny hours.

**Blog:**      countonlysunnyhours.wordpress.com
**Email:**    countonlysunnyhours5@gmail.com

**Gift:** Email me to receive a free copy of an excerpt from my memoir, *Count Only Sunny Hours*, my story of how I have travelled through grief to new life many times in my life. I am passionate about getting alongside hurting women, helping them learn resilience through life's adversity. I hope that by sharing how I bounced back from some very daunting experiences, I will inspire you to find the life you deserve.

## In the beginning

Living in The Hague in January 2011, I had finally made time to pursue a lifelong dream, which I hoped would stop the onset of middle age entirely engulfing me. I had always wanted to be a writer, and the title of my first book was hidden in my heart. Happily ensconced in lesson two of the 'Write Your Life Stories' workshop, I was confronted by my worst fear: proof of the extent to which computers have revolutionised other women's lives.

"If you want me to edit and help you publish your book, you need to be blogging," Jo, my dynamic writing mentor, kindly instructed.

"So what's blogging?" I asked, feeling like an almost extinct dinosaur in my IT illiteracy. I had started computer skills training but my learning pace was now excruciatingly slow. My previously excellent memory kept pressing *delete*, when I was not looking. On top of these learning challenges came my husband's latest relocation announcement.

"Good news, we're moving back to Qatar." I heard the relief in Andrew's voice as he eluded the threat of redundancy with plans for our third international move in four years. This was shortly before he disappeared to Doha, leaving me as a single parent for six months.

Cycling home to Leidschendam after writing class, nature reflected back my internal state of being. Flat, grey wetness created a fogginess that smothered the light as the clouds reached down to the canal. The tram-lined streets seemed full of gnarled arthritic tree limbs and dark, dank water. I shivered, feeling coldly soggy inside and out. Somewhere along the way, caring for my family and building new lives for everyone else, I seemed to have mislaid myself.

Six years ago in Qatar, my life was very different. I had created two part-time businesses I loved which provided an increasingly successful income. The challenges of being a counsellor were perfectly balanced with cuddling babies again in my parent-child swimming groups. Then surviving cancer immediately followed by moves to France and Holland took so much energy that years had suddenly passed.

Using my emerging computer skills, I had just discovered some online retraining opportunities, which would enable me to financially help my children reach for their dreams. I mused over what this would mean for me if I pursued the application. In September I would be moving continent, unpacking, setting up home, settling the kids in new schools, starting a postgraduate teaching certificate and a placement in a school all in fifty plus heat. Increasingly panicked by my ruminations, I accelerated too fast, wobbled alarmingly on my sitting-bolt-upright *omafiets* bike and almost toppled into the path of an oncoming tram.

Arriving home, I climbed the steep spiral steps to the newly created writing space in my bedroom. On top of a wooden IKEA table rescued from the garage sat a new PC notebook, a leaving vote of confidence from my husband. As I opened it up, my inner voices immediately started their cacophony.

"You haven't got time; your kids need you and what makes you think anyone will want to read your rubbish anyway?"

Passion for writing had erupted through the soil of my soul like the fresh green shoots of a tulip bulb with the promise of vibrant spring colour enfolded in its leaves. But would it wither and die away with the demands of a time-starving paid job?

The steepness of the learning curve I faced was like a ladder so tall it disappeared from view, making my tummy flutter and my brain complain, "I can't, it's too hard."

Could I let the upheaval of my fifth international move stop me pursuing my dream of becoming a writer?

## My Turning Point

I picked up a book from the pile of research material swamping my desk and Marianne Williamson's wisdom blazed through the stifling damp of my procrastination:

*Our deepest fear is not that we are inadequate. It is our light, not our darkness that most frightens us. Our deepest fear is that we are powerful beyond measure.*

Her words reminded me of my best cancer learned lesson: how I am living in time I thought I might never have and this ignites my determination to turn my writing dreams into reality.

---

**Taking stock**

At my Turning Point I knew my choices were...

- I could solve our financial deficits by starting a new teaching career in Doha.
- I could restart my counselling business in Doha.
- I could continue to let my lack of confidence in my computer skills disable my abilities and dreams.
- I could give in to the urge to give up.
- I could do nothing, enjoy a life of leisure in Doha and let my children pay their own university fees.
- I could decide that this time I can provide for my children, follow my dreams and do what I love.

---

## Making it happen

Opening a new Word document, I wrote the first line of my book "may my life-song sing to you". Writing is like spring arriving in my body, mind and soul, my favourite season. Despite the stresses of an international move, I continue to make time to write and will be taking all these fresh-start bulbs into the desert with me.

Freeing up time to do the things I love means that I no longer feel guilty about paying for a cleaner or saying no to coffee morning chats as I block off writing time. This is investing in me. Planning ahead to my fresh start in Doha, I am exploring teaching and counselling online qualifications, which could secure a future career, if I so choose. But this year and next year I will give myself the gift of time to write my book.

## My plan for improvement

I...

- researched distance PGCE courses and school placements.
- networked with counselling contacts in Doha to identify current private practice issues and opportunities.
- put myself into situations that would make me practise my computer skills such as setting up my blog myself and Internet banking.
- practised writing and received feedback by regularly blogging.
- used the time I had in Holland to take as many writing workshops as possible.
- continued computer skills lessons and applying new knowledge. I did it myself, not ask others to do it for me.
- prioritized writing now to get the framework of my book done by blocking off my diary to write.
- got more help at home and with the children to free up time.
- started up a creative writing support group in Holland and researched for Qatar.

## Moving forward my way

We do have choices, not necessarily in what happens to us, but in how we react, what we do with the challenges life sends our way. I am done with surviving and have started thriving again, blessed with an abundant freedom of choice. The rich tapestry of international writing women that have been divinely woven into my life is wealth beyond measure. I am finally thankful that computers are here to stay and we can be in touch, at the touch of a button.

## Wisdom from along the way

I have learned...

- Network, network, network for support, resources, information and updating.
- The Chinese word for 'crisis' is the same as for 'opportunity'.
- You are never too old to learn a new skill or change your mind.
- Remember who won the race; the tortoise got to the finish line first. You may be slower than you once were, but you will get there, one step at a time.
- Bad times are seasonal. Just like winter, they do pass into spring.
- Get help with the jobs you hate, to free up time for what you love doing.
- Surround yourself with soul mates. If people don't enrich your life you can edit them out.
- You reap what you sow, so be generous in paying on what you have been given to help others.

- There is a big difference between difficult and impossible.
- Keep remembering to breathe deeply.

## Resources to rave about

**Books**
*Release the Book Within* Jo Parfitt
(Lean Marketing Press, 2009)
If you are lucky enough to live in The Hague her inspiring writing workshops can be booked through Jo@joparfitt.com

*The Artist's Way: A Spiritual Path to Higher Creativity* Julia Cameron (Penguin Putman, 2002)

*The Resilience Doughnut: The Secret of Strong Kids* Lyn Worsley (Wild and Woolley, 2010) www.theresiliencedoughnut.com.au

*A Movable Marriage* Robin Pascoe
(Expatriate Press Ltd, 2005)

*The Gift of Change* Marianne Williamson
(HarperCollins, 2004)

# FROM PROFESSIONAL CROSSROADS TO A DIFFERENT ECONOMICS

## *MAY'S STORY*
## *COMMUNITY OF CHANGE*

### *NAME: MAY MOORE*

## About me

My story is all about 'the journey'. The passion for travel and discovery puts me in the category of 'archaeological-detective', but, for me, the desire is not to unearth *thing*s or *artefacts*, but people and places. The places? Too many to mention, but all of them mini-voyages contributing to the wider picture. As a trained lawyer and lecturer to international students in European law, corporate social responsibility and business ethics, I relish the daily contact with so many different cultures.

I campaign to change laws and am currently involved in arguments to change elderly care in the UK.

I now live between UK and France with my partner, who allowed me to share his fabulous children– that too, a voyage of its own standing!

**Website:** www.justchangeuk.org

## In the beginning

I was bored, very bored. I had surrendered a potentially successful law career, blaming my separation from my ex and the sale of our house as the excuse. Any job which followed such an exciting period of study and experience would be dull, and I found one with a charity with good objectives to bring education to those excluded by social class or disadvantage, but the people (save a couple of exceptions) and the main job tasks were dull nevertheless. Switching location from the City of London to an industrial estate on the Thames Estuary hit hard. Although my new family provided the internal comfort, a long stretch of dull employment years was not enthralling.

I was only 40, an only child – survivor of a mother with an undiagnosed, untreated mental illness, saved by a grounded father of intellect – with a passion for travel and adventure developed out of a rationale to run away. Born in London, to material comfort, I had a wonderful childhood. School days were spent enjoying academia and laughter in the playground. My post-university career in teaching, followed by a mid-career change into law, had created a network of inspirational people, so 'dull' was a challenging contrast. I have never been good at under-stimulation, and have a personality which rails against tedium by mischief-making. The work environment, for me, had always been a personal 'theatre'; far from being the nine to five, my working life had always been one of entertainment, stimulating people and challenges...up until now...

At yet another (dull) meeting, I sat next to a new colleague, to whom I chatted over lunch. This young, enthusiastic member of the team had just returned from what sounded an awe-inspiring adventure. He had spent one month on a charity project in India, observing and, where his skills allowed, assisting projects. The organisation, projects and people seemed more elevated, more earnest than the usual gap-year projects found on the internet. I did further research into Just Change India and, fully enthralled by the background of 'Development from the Inside', found myself booked on a flight to Bangalore, spending a month amongst unknown folk in unknown places.

Touching down in Bangalore, my senses were challenged by noise, smells and the sight of sacred cows causing traffic jams. When we reached Mysore, the kite-birds circling above our hotel were a daily reminder of the persistent presence of rotting flesh; if you die publically in India, be you animal or human, you remain public.

All of the projects were inspirational and unforgettable – the pioneering women starting up local co-operatives, making soap, trading chickens, the sex-workers' safe-house where prostitutes could find safe refuge, food and, if wanted, an alternative way to exist... but the visit which has energized me most was to a vast rural region of tea and pepper-growing, a stunningly wondrous region of Tamil Nadu, Gudalur.

At the heart of Just Change's operation, Gudalur has the feel of survival – there's a buzz of energy about the town and people. Here, we heard farmers' tales of near ruin and starvation brought about by commercial exploitation from multi-national companies, but one particular example of this now defines my future path.

A farmer, shaking with anger, told the tale of the 'destructor seed', a variety of seed purchased cheaply by poor farmers, which stops growing mid-cycle, needing the addition of expensive fertiliser – only available from the monopolistic pharmaceutical company which created the seed – to allow the process to complete – exploitation at its very worst as it caused crops to fail and trapped farmers into a web of expense on which their livelihoods depended.


## My Turning Point

The blind rage I felt, spending that day with farmers who were just surviving, flicked a switch onto a new outlook on global economics!

I walked away from that farm vowing that, as Just Change India advocates, anything I did from now on – projects worked on, ideas developed, items consumed or created – would not be at the expense of others: people, places, animals.

Through their own efforts and the intervention of Just Change India, those farmers are now independent of Western pharmaceutical exploitation, but many others are not.

How could I now just return to a comfortable, middle-class lifestyle in suburban UK?

---

**Taking stock**

At my Turning Point I knew my choices were…

- I could put the experience down to a 'significant' learning point.
- I could get despondent, bitter and internally angry at 'everything'.
- I could remain sad and ashamed at my part in the exploitation.
- Or, I could design a productive, positive path to honour those I had met.

---

## Making it happen

I returned from India with a new world view. The combined experience of Just Change India, not least the intellect of the directors, re-focused my energies and direction. Although unlikely that I would return to my beloved law practice, teaching law would satisfy my passion for the discipline by sharing it with others, especially those whom I could inspire to follow their career paths into the profession.

I was invited to help sixth form students select their university choices at one of the UK's top state grammar schools – a position, in turn, which exposed me to stimulating extra-curricular school activities: drama and music. An off-chance participation in a music project led to the most fabulous professional experience – an opportunity to start a registered charity which encourages singing in schools and promotes intercultural understanding.

## My plan for improvement

I...

- became more aware of what motivates and inspires me.
- continued to change and challenge elements of injustice – big and small.
- navigated a path which uses all my positive features, not the negative ones.
- acknowledged the negative features (the list is very long) and took small steps to improve them, accepting that I fail at this, sometimes.
- assisted those organisations whose core values are to challenge exploitation – people, animals, places.
- decided that when success had been achieved, I would share it with others.
- shared material comfort and surplus resources with those who either need it, or are challenging exploitation.

## Moving forward my way

Organising international singing events led to my current post as a university law lecturer within a multinational environment. I still travel the world, but each day my working environment, my classroom, contains representatives from the globe – I can 'travel' without a passport.

My contact with Stan and Mari at Just Change India continues, and I marvel as Mari travels the world campaigning for women's rights in Asia and writes for *The Guardian* and the *New Internationalist*. I have recently returned from another stay in India, this time to recruit students seeking access to education by studying degrees in the UK.

---

## Wisdom from along the way

I have learned…

- Accept that, sometimes, a period of working alone or freelance is required, and don't fear the challenge.
- Be open to the opportunities life throws at you – you never know where they may lead.
- Take a pro-active position about ONE thing; small changes which improve lives can magnify along the way by inspiring others to do the same.

# Resources to rave about

## Books

*Jane Eyre* Charlotte Bronte (Wordsworth Classics, 1992 (first published 1847)). An emblem of survival, courage, challenge

*Father and Son* Edmund Gosse (Oxford World Classics, 2004 (first published 1907)). An enigmatic tale of male relationships, conflicting value-systems, and love

## Organisations

38 Degrees, www.38Degrees.org.uk,
UK-based campaigning organisation

Just Change India, www.justchangeindia.org

Just Change UK (JCUK) has been set up as part of the international Just Change network, to tackle poverty and social exclusion in the UK through an innovative model of 'fair trade'.

Subscribe to the Just Change newsletter on
www.justchangeuk.org/newsletter/subscriptions
and buy tea to help the tea growers in India and to help create small businesses and jobs in UK at
www.justchangeuk.org/buytea

# Summary

## Five Key Things to Take Away

Here's a reminder of five key points that come out time and time again from the stories you have just read.

> ### 1.  Everything happens for a reason
> Even if we can't see what it is at the time or *never* understand its significance. All the challenges we face and overcome prepare us for the next adventure in life and make us stronger and better equipped to deal with it. The losses, the difficulties, the failures are just steps along the pathway, and the sooner we can learn from them, the sooner we can move on.

> ### 2.  The story is always about YOU
> Not about other people or circumstances around you. Take ownership for your decisions, your triumphs and your disasters and keep focused on your vision. Be honest with yourself and believe in yourself. Make your development a priority and don't be afraid to invest in training, coaches, mentors and anything else that helps you understand YOU, then share this with others.

### 3. Get help

Don't think you have to do it all on your own. You need a team around you to support and help you. Don't be afraid to ask for help and get others to do the jobs you hate so you are free to concentrate on what you love. Build a network of excellence around you and be prepared to return the favour when needed.

### 4. Be bold

Don't let fear of failure stop you and stand in your way. Think, make decisions and take action based on what you feel to be right for you and not what others tell you. Come from a place of love and be grateful.

### 5. Remember you can create your own future

You're already doing it so get conscious about it and create a *positive* future. Everything that you can envisage for yourself is possible and *can* come about so never abandon your dreams but turn them into reality.

# Women's Magic

Women  Cook
Women  Clean
Women  Glean
Women  Teach
Women  Preach
Women  Inspire

Women  Tire

Bogged down in the mire.

Women  Fret
Women  Fight
Women  Write
Women  Love
Women  Labour
Women  Lose

Women  Connect

Setting the world on fire.

*Sarah Koblow 12th May 2011*

# About the editor

Kate Cobb is Director of KC Consulting Ltd, a coaching and training company which focuses on leadership, communication and personal development work with organisations and individuals. A former senior manager in the public sector in UK, she has wide experience of consulting with private, public and not-for-profit organisations and as policy advisor and coach to senior managers. Her teaching assignments include MBA programmes with Institut Theseus, Sophia Antipolis, France and City University, London.

Kate specialises in working with women professionals who are ready for change and provides a variety of coaching and leadership programmes for them using blended learning methodologies.

Kate is an editor and writer and her publications include *Beginnings and Endings*, *10 Teambuilders* (Gower), *Indoor and Outdoor Team Development*, *Managing People through Redundancy*, *Mergers and Acquisitions* and *Practical Decision Making for Managers* (Fenman). She is an instructional designer and writes training programmes and materials for self study and delivery to groups. She regularly writes management and mentoring articles for magazines, on and offline.

As well as her consulting work in the business world, she uses her management skills in her community to organise orchestral, choral and operatic events.

Kate currently lives in the south of France, just outside Nice.


Contact details
kate@movingforwardyourway.com

# Seeds for Development

www.seedsfordevelopment.org

All we authors in this book appreciate how lucky we have been in our lives and we all wanted to 'pay it forward'. So Seeds for Development was the obvious choice of charity to support. The authors have personally made financial donations and these donations will buy quite a few seeds and help quite a few farmers and their families. In addition, 10 percent of the royalties from this book will be given to Seeds. In this way we can all assist others have their own Turning Points.

Seeds for Development is a small charity supporting the poorest people in Uganda. Its mission is to lift farmers out of poverty and support self-sustainability by providing risk free loans, in the form of agricultural inputs such as seed directly to the farmers.

It started in 2007 with an idea to help one family get out of grinding poverty. Today, it supports more than 700 farming families (around 7,000 people), working with them to move towards a happier and more hopeful life where they eat regular meals, send their children to school, build new and safer homes and even set up businesses.

The charity advances funds to farmers groups to buy seeds, tools and even wellington boots! They pay this back at the end of the season, meaning the money can be recycled the help more people. A bit like micro-finance without money, interest or risk!

The groups are carefully selected to ensure they are honest, hardworking and absolutely passionate about kicking poverty out of their lives, just as SfD is passionate about helping them.

SfD representatives try and personally meet the farmers, but with the number of groups growing all the time, this is not always possible. The main focus is in the post-conflict area of northern Uganda where there are many female-headed households who share motivation, enthusiasm and commitment to creating a better life for themselves and their children. They listen to, and learn from, the farmers ensuring that SfD supports them with what they need and not what we think they should have.

A handshake seals the agreement. Written contracts are signed by the Group committee on behalf of the farmers.

100% of donations go to the farmers. Seeds are not expensive, so our funds go a long way. For example, £35 will pay for bean seeds to cover one acre – the farmer can make over £300 from that acre of beans.

**Seeds for Development** was founded by Alison Hall in 2007, when, after hearing an inspirational talk by Ugandan business woman Josephine Okot, she had an idea to sponsor a farmer, rather in the same way you sponsor a child through school.

Now run by Alison with trustees; Sally Varley and Nicole Pickford, the charity supports more than 700 farming families in Uganda. They had no previous experience of Africa, charity work or agriculture!

**FARMER FEEDBACK**

"Since I left the camp my life has changed so much. I can now feed my family 3 meals per day but in the camp we could only eat once often waiting days for aid food. I could make no choices of my own. Now I have freedom. I can choose and plan my life and how my family eat, now that I know I have an income.

In the last month I have even been able to buy a bed for my children to share—now they don't have to sleep on the mud floor."

*Ellen, Parabongo IDP camp, 37 years old, married with 7 children*

For further information, contact Alison Hall
junipercottage@gmail.com

www.seedsfordevelopment.org

I met Alison Hall at the same Women's International Networking conference in 2010 where I met Jo Parfitt, our publisher, so that was quite an event. I was amazed to discover what this 'ordinary' corporate executive had achieved through her own Turning Point by founding Seeds for Development from nothing. I respect her enormously for her energy and enthusiasm. She's an example of what an individual can create when they are motivated and committed and a lesson to us all that our contribution to the world, however modest, can have great impact if we just get out there and do it!

Kate Cobb